Edna Lyall

Donovan

Vol. II

Edna Lyall

Donovan
Vol. II

ISBN/EAN: 9783337043810

Printed in Europe, USA, Canada, Australia, Japan

Cover: Foto ©ninafisch / pixelio.de

More available books at **www.hansebooks.com**

DONOVAN

A Novel

BY

E D N A   L Y A L L

AUTHOR OF

"WON BY WAITING."

"And I smiled to think God's greatness flowed around
                         Our incompleteness,—
Round our restlessness, His rest."
                E. B. BROWNING.

IN THREE VOLUMES.

VOL. II.

LONDON:
HURST AND BLACKETT, PUBLISHERS,
13, GREAT MARLBOROUGH STREET.
1882.

All rights reserved.

DONOVAN.

CHAPTER I.

CAST ADRIFT.

> Ruin's wheel has driven o'er us,
> Not a hope that dare attend,
> The wide world is all before us,
> But a world without a friend.
> BURNS.

> Two dry sticks will set on fire one green.
> He that takes the raven for a guide shall light upon carrion.
> *Eastern Proverbs.*

HOW long were things to go on in their present state? That was the question which, as the spring advanced, Ellis Farrant continually asked himself. One afternoon, towards the end of May, the thought pressed itself upon him more pertinaciously than ever. He was in the smoking-room, leaning back meditatively in his chair, from time to time reading a few lines in the *Sporting News*, but more often looking discontentedly and perplexedly at his step-son, who had drawn up his chair to the other side of the hearth, and whose fine profile was clearly marked out against the light as he bent over his newspaper. Two days ago Donovan had come of age, yet Ellis had not carried out his preconceived plan of revenge; in the past he had always intended to have the final breach with his step-son on the very day that his guardianship ended, but when the time actually came his heart failed him—no fitting opportunity presented itself. Instead of quarrelling with him, he drank his health at dinner, played billiards with him most of the evening, and was as good-natured and friendly as possible. But, although the few months which had elapsed since Dot's death had been singularly peaceable ones at the Manor, Ellis had not lost his strong dislike to Donovan. He had at first felt sorry for him, and had left him unmolested; but it is one thing to sympathise with a person in the first poignancy of his grief, and quite another to understand or feel for his prolonged sorrow.

As the months passed on, and Donovan's

grave stern face still remained unaltered, Ellis began to feel aggravated; he saw little enough of his step-son, but what he did see was quite sufficient to annoy him. Donovan would perhaps come down to breakfast, then he would disappear for the rest of the day, for long solitary rides or walks seemed to be his only relief; at dinner he would be in his place again, but would rarely utter a single word, and in the evening, though he was decidedly Ellis's superior at every game, he was too gloomy and taciturn to be a pleasant companion. The elder man's dislike and impatience began to grow uncontrollable; he found himself looking out eagerly for an opportunity of picking a quarrel.

As he sat looking thoughtfully across the room at his companion, his doubts were suddenly resolved by an unexpected turn of affairs. Donovan threw down his paper, and, turning round to his step-father, asked abruptly,

"When do you go up to town?"

"Next week, I believe," said Ellis, knocking the ashes out of his pipe and re-filling it.

There was a pause. Then Donovan continued,

"I have been thinking over things for the last few days, and I've made up my mind that this sort of life won't do for me any longer. I must begin to work at something."

"A most commendable decision," said Ellis. "And that's the longest sentence I've heard from you for many a month."

Donovan knew from the tone of this speech that his step-father was in a quarrelsome humour. He frowned, but continued, with some additional constraint in his manner,

"Since we are agreed, then, perhaps it would be as well if we arranged matters before leaving Oakdene. I am thinking of going into chambers and studying for the Bar; if you and my mother will settle my allowance, there is nothing that need keep me here longer."

"Gently, my good fellow," said Ellis, getting up from his chair with the feeling that he could carry things through with a high hand if he were standing above his step-son. "You are in rather too great a hurry; you rattle off in a few words what involves a great deal. I too have been thinking matters over, not only for the last two or three days, but for some time; by all means set to work if you like, only do not expect me to support you any longer. Live in chambers, if you will, and be a law-student for as many years as you please, only don't think that I shall keep you during the interval or pay your premium."

Donovan started to his feet.

"I don't understand you," he said, with repressed indignation. "What do you mean by this?"

"Simply what I say," said Ellis, provokingly.

"You mean me to understand that I am not to have any proper allowance made me?"

"Exactly so, though I don't admit the adjective."

The two men stood facing each other. For a few minutes neither spoke; Donovan's eyes dilated, and his face glowed with indignation. Ellis met his look with a cool bold effrontery.

At length the silence was broken by Donovan's voice.

"And *this* is what you have waited and plotted for! this is the part of the honourable English gentleman, to steal into a house, and win your way craftily, and mislead wilfully and shamefully those who never suspected your wickedness! Yes, you have fulfilled your duties as a guardian nobly, and now you would oust the 'insufferable cub,' whom you longed to kick out months ago, only you couldn't; instead you hoodwinked him, flattered, lured him on with false hopes. You *scoundrel!*"

"The step-son waxes hot," said Ellis, with a sneer, "as, naturally, we part this day, I will allow a few last shots."

"Wretch! Do you dare to turn me out of my own father's house?—you an interloper, a defrauder!"

"I have tolerated your presence in the house for ten months," said Ellis; "I knew that the time remaining was short, I let you stay on in peace; you have aggravated me at times beyond bearing, and now, with the greatest pleasure in life, I show you the door. You surmised quite truly, I have often longed to 'kick you out,' as you express it; take care that you do not force me to interpret the words literally."

"Do you think," said Donovan, angrily, "that my mother is so utterly unnatural that she will allow me to be treated in this way? I tell you you are mistaken, sir."

"You forget that your mother is my wife," said Ellis, watching his victim's writhing lip with a sort of enjoyment. "But, come now, I'll overlook what you've said, and we will part amicably; do not cut your own throat by refusing the pardon I offer."

"*Pardon!* And from you!" cried Donovan, passionately. "Am I to accept forgiveness for words which are a hundred times too mild for your conduct? I'll let the world know of the injustice, I'll publish your scandalous behaviour everywhere in the neighbourhood!"

"The only drawback to that scheme of revenge is the unfortunate character you yourself bear in the place," said Ellis, maliciously. "The neighbourhood will not very readily sympathise with any stories which the far-famed Donovan Farrant, the professed atheist, thinks fit to fabricate."

The statement was so true that Donovan could not deny it, but the consciousness of his utter isolation and the sense of injustice drove him almost to madness.

"That may be true!" he stormed, "anything may be true in a cruel, self-seeking, unjust world, but though everyone is against me, though I've not a creature on earth to hold out a hand to me, I will at least speak my mind to you. You are a traitor, sir, and a villain!"

"Take care," said Ellis, his colour mounting, "I give you fair warning that those words are actionable; use them again at your peril."

"You dare me to use them!" said Donovan,

furiously. "I will repeat them a thousand times—you are a treacherous, despicable villain! Were a hundred witnesses present, a hundred lawsuits possible, I would repeat it! What! am I to submit to be ruined without a word?—am I to sink down meekly into beggary because a plotting, scheming traitor like you dares to condemn me?"

Ellis was trembling with mingled fear and rage.

"You had better go while I can keep my hands off you," he said, fiercely. "Stay longer and I'll have you sent to Bedlam."

Donovan's brain seemed to reel; it was almost impossible to believe that he was actually being turned out of his father's house.

"I will see my mother," he said, with angry resolution in his voice. "She will not suffer it, she cannot."

He strode out of the room fiercely, and hurried across the hall to the dining-room. Waif, hearing his step, sprang up from the doormat and pattered after him, Ellis, following quickly, blocked the doorway before the door closed. Donovan turned back wildly.

"I tell you I *insist* on seeing my mother alone," he said, with a look so full of anger and hatred that Ellis shrank beneath it, but still he was able to answer with cold decision,

"And I tell you that I refuse to leave my wife with a maniac."

"Be it so," cried Donovan, "but, though you deny me everything, you cannot alter the instincts of nature. Mother, you will not—you cannot agree to this wickedness. You will not turn me away from this house penniless. You will not listen to what he says?"

Mrs. Farrant had been lying on the sofa; she started up from a doze to find the room in an uproar—Donovan and her husband storming at each other in a fashion without parallel. They had often before disagreed, even quarrelled in her presence, but in a quiet gentlemanly way, to which she did not object. This angry vociferation terrified her beyond measure. Donovan's rare and almost tropical outbursts of passion had always alarmed her. She turned now from his wild looks and impetuous words to her husband, who stood by in cold silence.

"What is the matter? What has happened, Ellis?" she asked, helplessly. "Pray stop this terrible noise. It is quite impossible for me to understand anything, Donovan, if you agitate me so."

"I will be quiet," he gasped, softening his voice with an effort. "I will not worry you for a moment. Only trust me, mother; listen to me fairly, and promise that you will not side against me. He—your husband insults me, drives me out of the house—this house which never ought to have been his—he turns me away penniless—say, only say that it is against your wish!"

Mrs. Farrant's tears began to flow, and she turned to her husband imploringly.

"Oh! Ellis, what has he done? Do not be hard upon him. He is the only child I have left. What has he done?"

Even in that moment of tumult, Donovan felt a thrill of joy at his mother's words. Was it possible that at last they might understand each other—that Nature would assert herself above the thick clouds of selfishness and uncongeniality which had so long divided them?

"Honora," said Ellis, in his coldest voice, "you must be content to trust me with this. I cannot allow Donovan's presence in my house any longer. For your sake I will let him go without calling him to account for the disgraceful language he has used to me, but go he must. He has been supported in idleness quite long enough; let him win his way in the world now as he can."

Donovan stood with his back against the window frame, and with arms folded, listening in silence to his step-father's words, listening, too, with painful intensity, for his mother's answer. Would she again plead for him, or would she be over-ruled by Ellis's cold speech?

"There has been nothing but trouble about him," sobbed Mrs. Farrant. "There seems to be a fate against me; nothing goes well. I have trouble after trouble. Oh! Donovan, why did you bring about this quarrel? For my sake you might have respected your step-father."

"At least believe that it was not my doing," cried Donovan, bitterly disappointed by her tone. "If you would only have believed what I told you last summer, we could not have been in this position; but who can stand against the coils of a serpent!"

"Go, sir," said Ellis, angrily, "go at once, and do not try my patience by upbraiding me before my wife."

"Did I not tell you that he would bring nothing but wretchedness to us?" said Donovan, desperately. "The time may come when you will see it more clearly. I can only hope that one victim may satisfy him, and that you may never suffer."

Mrs. Farrant sobbed convulsively, Donovan stooped down and kissed her, but, as he felt her tears wet on his cheek, he thought bitterly how one brave decided word from her would have been worth all this passionate sorrow.

With a dazzled bewildered feeling he crossed the hall and went up to his room; in a few minutes his bell was rung, and a message sent down to the housekeeper's room for Mrs. Doery to come upstairs. She came to him at once, looking so unchanged, with her nut-cracker features, sharp eyes, and respectable black dress and apron, that he felt almost as if time had been standing still with her, while it had brought such changes to him.

"Well, Mr. Donovan, what do you please to require?" she asked, severely.

He roused himself, and said in his natural voice—a rich mellow voice, but with a great ring of sadness in it—

"I am going away, Doery. Mr. Farrant has, in fact, turned me out of the house. I want you to put up my things for me."

Then, with that strange contradictoriness

whereby the very last persons in the world whom we expect to love us, suddenly reveal depths of unsuspected tenderness under the stress of some unusual event, Mrs. Doery broke into indignant sobs. She had never heard the like in her life! Turn her lad out of the house when he ought to have been made his father's heir! It was impossible, intolerable, she never would believe the law of England would allow it!

Her indignation rather softened Donovan, it was such a relief to feel that anyone, even this cross-grained old woman, would take his part! It seemed a strange reversal of the old order of things—Doery, stimulated by the cruelty of others, to allow some merit in him, or at least to bestow her pity on her ne'er-do-weel. He left her with a substantial souvenir, both for herself and for Dot's maid, Phœbe, generosity which in the precarious state of his finances was more natural than wise. Then he took a last look at Dot's room, put her little carriage clock with his own hands into his portmanteau, and leaving directions with Doery for his things to be sent to the Greyshot Station in time for an evening train, he went downstairs. Ellis was in the hall, waiting half nervously for the full accomplishment of his plans, for the crowning moment of his triumph. Donovan passed by him without speaking, deliberately took down his stick and riding-whip from the rack, and then, facing round upon his step-father, said with a depth of concentrated hatred and contempt,

"We part here, then. Remember always how admirably you have goaded me on to ruin!"

Then the door was closed behind him, and Donovan left the house which should have been his, and walked away alone.

It was a beautiful spring afternoon, the dark fir-trees and the early crimson of the copper beech stood out against the blue of the sky, the oaks were beginning to show their green leaves, the pink and white thorns were in full bloom. The beauty of the place seemed never to have been so great before, and though very often Donovan had thought the Manor dull and prison-like, yet now that he was exiled from it he found how large a place it had in his heart. And he was to leave it for ever! his home was to remain in the hands of his greatest enemy! At the first bend in the carriage drive he involuntarily turned back for a last look at the house. It stood there in the afternoon sunshine, with just the same air of sleepy luxurious comfort which it had always worn; there, above the creeper-laden porch, was the window of his old room, and close by it Dot's window. He remembered the day when he had decided to give up his foreign tour for the sake of being with her, and heard in fancy the childish voice which could never again call him; how strange now seemed the struggle of the past to give up his longing for a change of scene! how he grudged every hour that he had spent away from Dot! It was hard, very hard, to turn away from the place so full of her memory; no thought of future difficulties had as yet forced itself upon him, indignation and bitter sorrow drove out everything else—everything but a vague feeling of more complete desolation, more utter loneliness. He had thought that he had drained the full bitterness of the cup of life in the agony of bereavement, but here was a fresh draught which in its humiliating injustice was gall and wormwood to him.

All this time he was not however so friendless as he imagined; Waif followed him closely. His devotion to his master, which had always been very great, had become more marked since Dot's death; in Donovan's lonely rides and long walks Waif had always accompanied him, he had learnt to understand his master's moods and knew perfectly when to keep to heel in silent unobtrusiveness, and when to frisk and gambol about him; he had watched the stormy scene in the drawing-room, had followed Donovan noiselessly up and downstairs, now he trotted demurely behind him, well aware that this was not the right time to draw attention to his presence.

The gates were passed at length, and Donovan stood without in the white dusty road; he did not pause or hesitate or look back now, but strode along with fierce rapid steps, down the hill, through the little village, past old Mr. Hayes' deserted house, to the tiny grey church in the valley. Everything looked cruelly peaceful, on the hillside a herd of cows were browsing, a column of blue smoke curled up from the chimney of a little farmhouse close by, a country woman passed him singing to the brown-eyed baby in her arms. Contrasted with all this were Ellis's cruel words ringing in his ears, and the recollection of the hateful look of vindictive triumph which he had seen in his step-father's face. The frenzied passionate indignation surged up in his heart with redoubled force, he threw open the churchyard gate, and hurried up the flagged path, pausing however beside the little porch to look at a notice which had met his eye, as trifling things do sometimes force themselves upon us in moments of great agitation. He read with growing bitterness the words :—

"NEW ORGAN FUND.—Ellis Farrant, Esq., of Oakdene Manor, having generously promised £200 to the above fund, it is earnestly hoped that the additional £100 still required may be obtained. A special collection will be made, &c., &c." Charity, church-organs, generosity to win a good name with the world! behind the outward show, injustice, tyranny, and hatred!

Donovan turned aside past the great yew tree to the place where little Dot had been laid. The stone had just been put up, a recumbent cross, the sharp outlines of the white marble standing out clearly against the green grass; he threw himself down upon it in one of his terrible paroxysms of grief, in pain so unalleviated that it seemed like strong physical torture added to the mental suffering. How long he lay there with his face pressed down to the cold marble, and his hands grasping strainedly at the turf he never knew; it must have been for a long long time, for when he staggered to

VOL. II. C

his feet again the sun was setting, and he found that only by walking briskly could he reach Greyshot in time for the evening train to London. With a still white cold face, which seemed to have absorbed something of the hard rigidity of the marble cross, he looked his last at the little grave, then hastily recrossed the churchyard. Waif, who had been watching him all the time with considerable anxiety, trotted on in front of him, but at the gate turned back to meet him and began to draw attention to himself by a series of whines and barks and bounds in the air; he could not have chosen a better moment for making his presence known, Donovan felt at once the relieved re-action from hard bitter despair to a half-amused gratitude; this dumb creature loved him, there could be no doubt of that, and there are times in the lives of most of us, when the love even of dumb things wins a tenfold preciousness because of its unquestioning faithfulness, its fearless devotion, its contrast to the changeful doubting unreliable affection of men, who can judge and speak their judgment. He stooped down and let the dog spring up to his knee, while he patted the sagacious white and tan head; then, remembering that his time was short, he started up again with a sudden return of energy.

"Come along, old fellow," he said, in his usual voice, "you and I will go through the world together."

Waif wagged his tail, pricked up his black ear, drooped the white one, and bounded along as if he enjoyed the thought of the companionship.

It was growing dusk when the dog and his master reached Greyshot; the station lamps were lighted; somehow Donovan's choking indignation began to diminish under the influence of the excitement. He had been unjustly used, certainly, but the world was before him, and the world began to seem more attractive than he had thought; the cool evening wind blew through the station, the platform was rather crowded, for the first time a boyish sense of the pleasure of freedom stole across him; here he was accountable to no one, free to do exactly as he pleased, with his portmanteau and his dog he could roam where he liked. He took a ticket for himself and Waif to Paddington without any very distinct idea why he chose London as his first resort, turning to it perhaps only as the sort of natural home which the great city seems to most Englishmen.

Then he sauntered up and down, waiting for the train, looked at the brightly lighted bookstall, scanned the faces of the crowd, while all the time his thoughts were running pretty much in this way:

"I must make the best of life; hateful and worthless as it is, I may as well enjoy myself as much as I can. The world is full of injustice, I will pay it back in its own coin."

Presently the train was heard in the distance, in another minute his golden-eyed destiny flashed into sight, there was haste and confusion on the platform. Waif, with his ticket tied to his collar, kept close to his master's heels, till Donovan, opening the door of a carriage, prepared to lift him in; the occupants, however, objected, a nervous middle aged lady started up from her corner, she could not endure dogs, she really must beg that he did not get into that carriage. Donovan retreated, and hurried on to the next vacant place, taking care this time to put the question,

"Do you mind the dog?"

"Oh, dear no," said a pleasant bland voice, and he sprang in just as the train started.

When he had put up his bag and walking-stick, he threw himself back in a corner seat, and began to scrutinize his fellow-passengers. They were three in number, and they were beguiling the time with a game of euchre. The individual with the pleasant voice, who had consented to Waif's admittance, sat next to Donovan, so that he could only see his profile; he seemed to be a short, heavily-made man between fifty and sixty, with an unnaturally red face, thick neck, and scanty red hair sprinkled with grey; he was singularly ugly, but his expression was more weak than unpleasant, especially when he turned round with some trifling remark to Donovan, and showed his little twinkling watery eyes, good-natured mouth, and round face. His two companions were much younger men, the one furthest from Donovan was faring badly in the game, he was a sleek-looking, bearded man, dressed rather extravagantly, and wearing a heavy watchchain and bunch of charms; there was an air of vulgar prosperity about him, and Donovan instantly surmised that he was some wealthy manufacturer or tradesman. The remaining traveller was a much more perplexing study. After watching him for some time, Donovan had not in the least arrived at any decision about him, he might have been a sporting gentleman, or a superior commercial traveller, or a newspaper correspondent, or possibly a card-sharper. Donovan tried to fit every one of these "callings" upon him; each succeeded for a time, and then fell to the ground. He was, however, peculiarly attractive. His companions were very soon forgotten altogether in the absorbing interest of watching this man's exceedingly clever play and curious face. He had a square massive forehead, black hair receding from the temples, and just beginning to turn grey, a dark oily complexion, very small black eyes, with a dissatisfied look in them, and heavy dark eyebrows, level towards the bridge of the nose, but arched at the other end, and raised still higher when he became interested.

Before very long the manufacturer was beaten, and the dark-browed man turned to Donovan, shuffling the cards as he spoke.

"Will you make a fourth at whist?"

The question was asked so casually, as if the speaker cared little whether he complied or not, that Donovan, who had rather inclined to the opinion that he *was* a professional gambler, was completely deceived by it. He only hesitated a moment, then the red-haired elder man turned round with his good-humoured smile, and said, in his pleasant voice,

"We should be delighted, if you would join us. One needs something of the sort on a long journey, to while away the time."

Without further preamble the game began. The stakes were high; Donovan grew excited, and forgot for the time his anger and the bitter treatment to which he had been subjected. He was partner with the rich manufacturer; the strange-looking, dark-browed man was playing with the elder with the red hair. He was a daring opponent, and Donovan, who was accustomed to carry everything before him, was roused and interested to a most unwonted degree. It was a close and exciting game, eventually won by the two strangers, but Donovan's skilful play had evidently surprised his dark-looking opponent, who scrutinized him curiously, while the red-haired traveller began to compliment him.

Presently they stopped at Swindon, and Donovan, beginning to be conscious that he had eaten nothing for many hours, hurried away with the others towards the refreshment-room. As he waited for an instant among the crowd of passengers, he heard a sharp voice, low, and yet singularly distinct, not far from him.

"Now mind, your work's not done yet, so be careful."

Glancing round, Donovan saw that the speaker was his late opponent; the good-humoured face of his red-haired companion clouded a little, and there was something of the expression of a spoilt child about his mouth as he replied.

"Plague upon it! You never can let a fellow enjoy himself, Noir. I'm sure I've been as temperate as old Oliver himself——"

The rest of the sentence died away in the distance, but apparently Noir enforced his advice, for, some minutes before Donovan left the refreshment-room, his two fellow-travellers repassed him on their way to the carriage.

Waif sat guarding his master's property. The two men did not notice him; the younger one, who had been addressed as Noir, flung himself back in his place, the elder fidgeted about restlessly, talking in his hearty voice the while.

"What do you think of our two friends?"

"The manufacturer is a fool," said Noir, decidedly. "The young one's as sharp as a needle."

"Ha! I thought as much. He'd have beaten us hollow, wouldn't he, if it hadn't been for certain——"

"Be quiet!" said the younger man, sharply. "You'll undo us some day by your want of caution."

"Shall you try any more this evening?"

"I don't know. I think not. I wish I could get that young fellow for a second instead of you. He'd be the making of us."

"A cut above our sort of thing, isn't he?"

"Can't say, but he looks discontented enough. We'll sound him, get the manufacturer to draw him out."

Then, as the other traveller returned, Noir suddenly changed his tone, and very skilfully drew the conversation round to the desired subject. They had just been talking of his partner. He seemed a clever fellow. They were wondering what he was. For his part, he would bet ten to one that he was in the Army. The manufacturer thought he was an undergraduate. There was some laughter over the dispute. It was agreed that, by hook or by crook, they would find out which was in the right by the end of the journey. Then the bell sounded. There was hurrying to and fro on the platform, and at the very last moment Donovan stalked back to his place, perfectly unconscious of the small plot which his companions had been making.

He had brought back a biscuit for Waif, and the dog made a good opening for conversation. Then the manufacturer mentioned by chance that he came *from Bristol*, and Donovan, to the satisfaction of the three conspirators, began to ask questions as to the likelihood of finding any suitable employment there.

"Oh! with capital, you can always get on," said the rich man, easily. "Nothing can be done in this world without money, but there are plenty of openings there for any young men wanting employment."

"Provided they are capitalists," said Donovan, with bitterness, which did not escape Noir's keen observance.

"Oh! well, of course you might meet with a clerkship," said the manufacturer, "but it's a difficulty to get them very often, there's such a run on them; and besides, that would hardly be in your line, would it?"

"No," said Donovan, haughtily; then, with a touch of humour, he added, "Though, to be sure, I've not much right to talk of 'my line.'"

The talk drifted on by degrees to the recent strikes in Lancashire, and the manufacturer and Donovan had a hot argument on the subject of wages, in which the latter's keen sense of injustice and oppression was fully brought to light; he talked so fiercely of the tyranny of the rich, the grinding down of the poor, the dishonest grasping of the capitalists, that Noir felt sure there was some personal feeling involved in the dispute, certain that in some way this young fellow's life had been embittered by the tyranny and injustice which he inveighed against. The dark brows were raised higher and higher as the argument went on; evidently Donovan's words had touched some kindred feeling in the man's heart. At last he could contain himself no longer, but joined in the dispute, linking his vehement words with Donovan's, till between them they fairly overwhelmed the rich Bristol man. Then at once there was established between them that strange sympathy which comes like a lightning flash, when two minds are entirely one upon a subject not usually agreed upon. They had been united in argument, and in an argument very nearly touching their own lives; instinctively Donovan held out his hand when they parted at Paddington, and the dark-browed man grasped it with a warmth and heartiness curiously contradictory to his disposition. He was in reality a hardened cheat, but his one vulnerable spot had been touched, and he at once conceived a strong liking for his young ally.

Perhaps few places are so dependent on the frame of mind one is in as London. No place seems so pleasant to a sociable person in a happy humour, no place so cold and uncongenial to anyone in trouble. Then with what heartless indifference the busy crowd passes by, how the careless talk, the hearty laugh, the cool stare of one's kind wound and sting; with what envy does one look at the smiling faces, and how (foolishly and morbidly, of course) one compares them with the priest and the Levite in the parable; though how they can help "passing by on the other side," when one is only stripped and wounded and robbed by the unseen foes of life which prey on the inner man, a troubled mind, is generally too illogical to consider. The forlornness of his position did not come upon Donovan all at once. During the months which had passed since little Dot's death, in his sorrow "without hope," worthier and more manly thoughts had grown up in his heart; he had made up his mind to work at something, and, though his chief object had been merely to divert his thoughts by the work, the resolve was still in the right direction. The rude repulse which he had met with from Ellis when he suggested his new idea, and the hardness of his expulsion from Oakdene, crushed down for the time all these better thoughts; but in a little while, from sheer necessity, they sprang up again. It was evidently impossible that he could live for any length of time on the remains of his last allowance; he must gain his living in some way, and now, for the first time, he felt fully how fatal to his interests Ellis's guardianship had been. Had he been forced to enter some profession, or had he even received a better education after his school career was ended, he would not now have been so helpless; yet, after all, he would scarcely have consented to leave Dot, even had he known beforehand of Ellis's malignant intention; only now it added bitterness to his indignation to think how coolly and systematically his step-father had planned his ruin. Why was it?—what had he done to earn such hatred? He asked himself those questions over and over again, knowing nothing of the first great wrong which Ellis had done him—the wrong which was at the root of all the subsequent evil.

The morning after his arrival he hurried off at once to Bedford Row to consult his father's solicitor, the same who had come down to his grandfather's funeral, and had initiated him into the mysteries of *vingt-et-un*. He was by this time an elderly man; but though he listened to Donovan kindly, and refused to take any fee for the consultation, he showed him at once that he had no legal claim whatever on Ellis Farrant or his mother now that he was of age. His case was no doubt a very hard one; he should think that by continued applications he might reasonably expect to extort some allowance, if only a small one, from his step-father. As to his mother, she had no power at all apart from her husband; he could take counsel's opinion if he liked, but it would be simply throwing away his two guineas—it was a matter quite out of the province of law, a family matter which must be arranged by family feeling and natural affection. As to employment, he should advise him to apply to any influential men he knew in town; it was possible he might get some post in one of the Government offices.

The lawyer hoped that Mr. Farrant would dine with him some evening—he had just moved to a new house at Brompton; if he could ever be of any service to Mr. Farrant, he should be most happy.

Donovan went away several degrees more depressed than before. His prospects did indeed seem dreary; "continued applications" to Ellis Farrant, or, in plain English, "begging letters," could not for a moment be thought of, and the lawyer's kindness failed to impress him. It was easy enough to ask a fellow to dinner, and to hold out vague offers of service; but Donovan had seen too hollow a corner of the world to put any faith in this sort of friendship. He resolved, however, to call on two or three great men whom in the old times he and his mother had visited; his name at least would be known to them. He would at any rate follow the lawyer's advice, and try for work. But each effort was doomed to fail. The first of the old acquaintance was kind indeed, but not encouraging; he knew of nothing in the least suitable, regretted extremely his inability to help his young friend. The second flattered him, assured him that with such advantages he could not fail to get on in the world, and promised that if ever he heard of any appointment likely to suit him he would let him know at once. The third, an overwrought man, always oppressed by twice as much work as he could properly manage, received him with scant courtesy, listened to his story coldly, and dismissed him with a curt refusal; it was no use coming to him, he had a thousand applications of the kind—they were, in fact, the bane of his existence. He could offer no help at all—he wished Mr. Farrant good day.

It was not till the close of this third interview that Donovan altogether realised his position. With hot cheeks, for he was still young enough to flush easily at any discourtesy, he turned his back on the chambers of the harassed and churlish man of the world, made his way along the crowded pavements of Parliament Street, and without any distinct purpose bent his steps towards the river. It was a hot afternoon in early June, but what little air there was reached him as he leant on the parapet of Westminster Bridge, his face propped between both hands, his eyes bent down on the sparkling sunlit water. What was the use of his life? he asked himself dejectedly. How indeed was he to live? His acquaintances one and all refused or were not able to help him, his home ties were all broken, there was not a single being in the world who would help him or care for him. Under such circumstances, would it not be well to seek that "refuge in the cavern of cold death" which he had taught himself to consider as the goal, the end of all things? What harm could it do to anyone? There was no one to miss him except Waif, and not to be would be ineffable peace! No more craving for Dot's presence, no more gnawing disappointment and weariness of life, no more suffering from injustice, no more misery of loneliness. And yet—— What would his father have said? And then, too, was there not some natural physical shrinking from such an end? After all, he was very young, and the boy-life within him began to assert itself above the morbid overgrowth. Life as it was, was certainly not worth having, but surely there must be some brightness in store for him! The sun shone down in golden splendour on the river, the pleasure-steamers and the smaller boats were borne past him rapidly; the mere animal joy of existence overcame for the time his darker thoughts.

Yet what was he to do? He did not know

the Bible well, but he had of course heard it read in his school days and before he gave up church-going, now from some odd recess of memory there floated back the words—" Make to yourselves friends of the mammon of unrighteousness that when ye fail they may receive you into everlasting habitations." He smiled a little to himself as he thought of the solution of this perplexing passage which his life was bringing to light. He had certainly taken no pains in the old days to make friends; where he could have wished friendship there had always been a shrinking back on the other side; his bad name had kept back good companions; his natural nobility had guarded him from making real friends of bad people, although he had been in the way of evil companionship very often. But a real friend he had never known. Certainly his circumstances were sufficiently dreary to have brought to despair a far better regulated mind than his; the misery and hopelessness surged in upon him afresh, the healthy pleasure in existence died away, the brightness of the summer day only increased his sick longing for something to fill the emptiness of his life.

Just as he had slowly raised himself and was

about to move on from the place where he had been leaning, he heard himself addressed in a voice which, though not exactly familiar to him, he yet seemed to have heard somewhere.

"Good day, I think we've had the pleasure of meeting before."

Turning round hastily, he at once recognized the dark-browed man with whom he had travelled up from Greyshot, his antagonist in the game, his ally in the argument.

"I've been watching you for some minutes," said the stranger, "only you seemed so deep in meditation that I wouldn't disturb you. I've often thought of you since that day we met on the Great Western."

"Have you?" said Donovan, brightening a little, for the man's manner had a certain attractiveness in it; then, after a moment's pause, he added, "Why, I wonder?"

"Why?" repeated the stranger, "because I like you, and it is so seldom I do like anyone that naturally, from the very oddity of the thing, I thought of you."

They had moved on while talking, and now, leaving the bridge, walked along the embankment. Donovan liked the man, and yet was too reserved and too prudent to care to make any advances to him. The stranger began to see that he must take the initiative.

"Have you found the work you were looking out for?" he asked, turning his dark restless eyes on his companion.

Donovan shook his head, all his despondency returning at this allusion.

"I thought as much from your look," said the stranger. "You haven't found it such an easy matter as you expected. If you are hard up though, it is just possible that I may know of employment which would suit you."

"You! Do you indeed?" cried Donovan, eagerly. "But perhaps I shan't be up to it; I don't mind telling you that, up to a very little time ago, I never dreamed that I should have to work for my living; now, through a great injustice, I am on my own hook, with only a five-pound note between me and beggary."

"So bad as that," said the stranger, thoughtfully, "then perhaps you will not be too scrupulous for the work I was thinking of; you are certainly well cut out for it. Look! If I treat you with entire confidence and openness, may I take it for granted that you will not abuse my trust?"

"Of course," said Donovan, growing interested.

"If you will come with me, then, to my rooms, I will explain the sort of work which I mean, you will not of course be bound to accept it if you don't like it. My name is Frewin; the old man you met with me the other night is my father; we are generally called *Rouge et Noir*."

Donovan smiled at the singular appropriateness of the nickname. The stranger continued,

"That you may believe me, I will tell you that it is not all from disinterested motives that I seek you out and try to help you, no one in the world goes upon such motives, self-interest is the great ruling principle; you are admirably suited to help me in my work, that is my first reason; I like you and am sorry for you, that is my second. Now I have made a clean breast of it all, will you come?"

"Of course I will," said Donovan, without an instant's hesitation. He committed himself to nothing by this, why should he not go? And besides, these were the first helpful friendly words which he had heard for so long.

CHAPTER II.

ROUGE ET NOIR.

> The fall thou darest to despise—
> May be the angel's slackened hand
> Has suffered it that he may rise
> And take a firmer, surer stand;
> Or, trusting less to earthly things,
> May henceforth learn to use his wings.
>
> And judge none lost, but wait and see
> With hopeful pity, not disdain,
> The depth of the abyss may be
> The measure of the height of pain,
> And love and glory that may raise
> This soul to God in after-days.
>
> A. A. PROCTER.

NOIR FREWIN took his companion up one of the narrow streets leading from the river, along the Strand as far as St. Mary's Church, and through the dingy foot-passage opening into Drury Lane.

"This is not what you have been accustomed to, I expect," he said, taking a quick glance at

Donovan's face. "I suppose you've been putting up at some tip-top hotel by way of economising."

Donovan coloured a little, for the surmise was true enough, but there was nothing impertinent in the man's tone, and he added,

"You'll learn differently as you see more of life. I've lived in Drury Lane on and off now for five years, and am in no hurry to leave the old place, dirty as it is. Here we are!" and he stopped at the private door of a dingy picture-dealer's shop, admitted himself and Donovan, and led the way up a dark staircase to the first floor.

Expecting a room of corresponding dinginess and dirtiness, Donovan was not a little surprised to find himself in a snug neatly-arranged room, where an odd combination of a variety of the brightest colours lent an almost Eastern look to the whole. Curious shells and corals were ranged on shelves along the walls, maps and nautical charts hung in conspicuous places, a case of gorgeous foreign birds occupied the entire length of the room, and a live parrot, in a brass cage, hung in one of the windows, looking at the new-comers with his shrewd, questioning, round eyes. Leaning back in a smoking-chair, absorbed in a newspaper, and with a long clay pipe between his lips, was old Rouge Frewin, no longer in the irreproachable suit which Donovan had first seen him in, but wearing a rough blue serge jacket and red-tasselled cap. He hurried forward at a word from Noir with more than his former heartiness and good humour.

"Delighted to see you, sir. How has the world gone with you since we parted? I must introduce myself to you as Captain Frewin, unless, perhaps, my son has already done so, Captain Frewin, formerly of the steamer *Astick*, Bright Star Line, carrying between Liverpool and New York, latterly of the *Metora*—first-rate little steamer she was, too—carrying between Southampton and West Africa."

Donovan could hardly keep his countenance, the whole scene was so irresistibly comic, the funny old sea-captain, in his red smoking-cap, gesticulating with his long clay pipe, the odd room, and the sudden burst of confidence which had revealed the history of its owner. But his face clouded again as Rouge asked him the same question as to his success in finding work which Noir had put to him on the embankment.

He had only just begun his dispirited answer,

however, when he was interrupted by a loud nasal voice, which screamed out, "Keep up your pecker! keep up your pecker!" and glancing round he met the goggle eyes of the parrot. It was too much for the gravity even of depressed, ruined, ill-used Donovan, he burst out laughing, a natural, hearty, boyish laugh, such as he had not enjoyed for many months.

"You see Sweepstakes encourages you," said Noir, tormenting the bird by thrusting a piece of string through the wires of its cage.

"What's its name?" asked Donovan, still laughing.

"Sweepstakes, we call him," said old Rouge, coming to the rescue of his pet. "I've had him for seven years, we're great friends, aren't we, Sweepstakes?"

"Poor Sweepstakes!" said the bird, with its head on one side. "Poor Sweepstakes! 'Weep, 'weep, 'weep," and he broke off into an exact imitation of the street cry.

"We have a little business to talk over," said Noir, when the parrot subsided at last. "Suppose," turning to Rouge, "you were to go to Olliver's and order dinner for three in half an hour, and we'll meet you there. You won't refuse to dine with us, I hope," he added, glancing at Donovan.

"Oh! no," said Rouge, heartily. "You mustn't do that. Besides, I've not half shown you round our little cabin. I'm very proud of my curiosities, I can assure you. The bird has evidently taken to you already. You must make yourself quite at home."

As soon as the door had closed behind the old man, Noir Frewin drew up a chair for his guest, and seating himself opposite, with his elbows planted on the table, and his chin between his hands, said,

"And now, if you've the patience to listen, I will tell you a story. I shall trouble you with some account of my own life, because only by that can I show you why it is I take an interest in you. I hate most of the world. I should hate you, if you weren't unfortunate, but I see you are in some way the victim of injustice, and, as I told you before, I like you. Bear with me a little. This will all help to explain the work I propose for you.

"My father, as he told you, was once the captain of a mail-steamer. He was, of course, absent most of the year. I lived with my mother, and as soon as I left school got a clerkship in a bank at a town—no matter in what county. Things went very smoothly with us for a long time, and at last my father, who is a very warm-hearted man and hated being away from his home, thought he had saved enough to retire and settle down in England. He resigned his ship, and for a few months we lived on happily enough. I was as contented a fellow then as you'd often meet with. I liked my work, and received a good salary; moreover I was engaged to be married, and the future looked—well, no matter. I lived in the usual fool's paradise of a lover." He paused a moment, as if reviewing from the distance the old happiness, then, with a bitter sneer, he continued: "Of course I paid dearly for all this foolishness. I don't think I was a bad fellow in those days; goodness knows I'd no excuse for being so, for my mother was the best woman in the world. However, though I did well enough then, I couldn't stand the hard times that followed. There was a grand row one day at the bank, for it was found that by some forgery a cheque for one hundred pounds had been unlawfully abstracted. Suspicion fell on all those connected with the bank, and it narrowed down, as such things do, till it was clearly proved that either I myself or the son of the manager had done the deed. Of course I had not done it—the truth came to light later on—but at the time everything seemed against me, and since the manager was not a second Brutus he was naturally inclined to believe his son in the right. I don't care to go into all the misery of that time. There was, of course, a mockery of a trial. I was found guilty, and the real perpetrator of the forgery sat in court, and heard me condemned. I saw him turn pale when he heard me sentenced to seven years penal servitude—perhaps, though, he was only thinking of the danger he had escaped."

"But did he make no effort to save you?" questioned Donovan. "I shouldn't have thought a man could have been such an utter brute."

"You have yet to learn the world, then?" said Noir, with a fierce laugh. "Oh! yes, of course he was kind enough to do all in his power to get me recommended to mercy. I think he hoped for a lighter sentence. However, what difference did it make to me? I was sent to Pentonville, and there I ate my heart for a year. Then I was sent to Dartmoor, and I think the change just saved me from madness. That year my mother died.

We had been everything to each other. She couldn't stand the disgrace which had come to us, or the separation. I was young, and had to stand it, but I think from that day I wasn't the same fellow. The next thing which happened made me ten degrees worse. In one of my father's letters—letters are very few and far between in convict life—I learnt that the girl I had been engaged to was married to another. I told you I paid dearly for my fool's paradise. After that I didn't care what happened. Of course I had lost my character, and I knew that it would be next to impossible for me to get any situation when my term was over. I made a friend at Dartmoor, a fellow of the name of Legge, a clever man, too, and good-natured. We came out at the same time, and he helped me on a little. But things were worse even than I had fancied. My father, in his trouble and loneliness, had fallen into bad ways. I found that in my seven years' absence he had become a confirmed drunkard. You can fancy what a return that was! I could get no employment, and at last, with Legge's help, I began to practise my present profession."

"You mean the profession you practised in the train the other night?" said Donovan.

"Precisely," rejoined Noir, "and I've made it answer. People may say what they like, but the world's one great cheat, and I delight in taking it in unexpectedly. It has ruined me, why may not I get a little out of it in return! I told you though that the truth would come to light, and my innocence came to light in time, though I didn't care a straw about it then. A year after I was released from Dartmoor I was traced out with some difficulty by the manager of the bank, his son had just died and confessed to the forgery. The manager tried to express his great shame and sorrow, hoped he could make some reparation for the injury, offered me money—think of that! Money to make up for the ruin of a whole life! I told him there could be no reparation—that if he would bring back my mother from the grave, if he would reclaim my father, if he would restore me my betrothed, if he would give me back those wasted seven years, and give me again the faith in God and man which had been beaten out of me by the maddening injustice, then, and only then, could he repair the injury."

"I'm glad you've told me all," said Donovan, when the narrator paused; "yours is a hard story certainly, bitterly hard. How long is it since you were released?"

"Five years," said Noir, relapsing into his ordinary tone, a quiet cold tone, very different from the one in which he had recounted his wrongs. "I have lived here with my father chiefly, trying to keep him in order, but it's a hopeless task, where the taste is once acquired it's almost impossible for a weak-minded person to cure himself. I have lived on, making money in the way I told you, and the other day when you got in at the Greyshot Station, there was something in the look of you that attracted me. Then you played uncommonly well, and for the first time in my life I felt sorry that I was cheating a fellow. Afterwards when you talked to that capitalist, I took to you still more; my father had so often been more of a hindrance than a help, and I couldn't help thinking what a capital second you would make. That is the work I propose for you. You should of course have a certain percentage of the profits, and if you live with us, all the better; there's a room at the back which you could have, and though I suppose it's a very different life from what you've been used to, still you might do worse, and

I can promise you what I couldn't promise to another fellow in the world—real honest liking. Perhaps you will say the friendship of a professional gambler isn't worth having; however, such as it is I offer it to you, sometimes anything is better than nothing. No, don't give me an answer yet. We'll have dinner now, and you can think things over for a day or two, and let me know."

Had Donovan given his answer then, it would probably have been a refusal, but he went to the Frewins' club, listened to the captain's long yarns, grew doubly interested in Noir, and had a series of brilliant successes at the card-table. Then he went home—that is to his hotel, to think over the offer that had been made to him. All that night he struggled with his perplexities. On the one hand were his rich acquaintances coolly, if civilly, refusing to help him, on the other was the open hospitality and friendliness of the Frewins; midway between the two his conscience put in a plea for a further search after honest work. In his heart of course he disapproved of the proposed scheme, but his principles of right and wrong were somewhat elastic, and just now in his anger and misery, the good within him was at a very low ebb. Moreover, it was true enough, that these Frewins were the only people who had shown him any kindness, and naturally he caught at the sympathy and liking of even a bad man, when it was the only thing to be had; it was like the old familiar saying of a drowning man catching at a straw; he may know well enough that the straw is frail and hollow, but it is something to lay hold of, if only for a moment, and in the absence of a better support it seems worth clinging to.

To say that he made the choice while he was unconscious of its evil would not be true; some people are so ready to admit excuses, there are always so many extenuating circumstances, or states of mind or body which account for the fall, that very few sins are put under the head of " Wilful." But in after years Donovan never allowed that he had taken the step unconsciously. Of course sin, taken in its usual sense, did not now exist for him, but he was perfectly aware that he was entering upon a wrong and immoral course; he made the false step desperately perhaps, but deliberately. The very last words he had had with Noir Frewin were sufficient to prove this.

"I may ask your name now?" the man had

said, as they parted. And Donovan, for the first time in his life, had shrunk from giving it; how could he let his father's name become the name of a—but there he checked even his thoughts, and hastily gave only his Christian name.

For a little while he thought things over, as Noir had suggested; it was true there were ways and means of raising money, but, even if he had had good security to offer, he would not have cared to put himself into the hands of a money-lender. Or there was another alternative; he had heard Mr. Probyn, Ellis Farrant's friend, relate proudly the length of time he had lived "on tick," as he called it—this was most likely the course which would have been chosen by nine persons out of ten, had they been placed in his predicament,—but there was nothing to commend this expedient to him, living in debt was simply robbing tradespeople, there could be no doubt of that; if he must live by chicanery, he might as well do so in a more amusing way than by a skilful eluding of duns, and it was better to cheat fools who chose to risk their money in a game than honest shopkeepers. Thus he argued with himself, what his school-fellows had called "his crazy ideas of honour" coming out strongly; but he held fast to his theory, and never had a single debt. The true and honest course never once entered into his head; if he had had sufficient humility to visit his father's solicitor again and beg his assistance, in all probability he would have been helped, for in such an extreme case people are often kind-hearted enough; but absolutely to throw himself on anyone's mercy was simply impossible to Donovan—he was at once too proud and too distrustful of human nature.

The consideration ended, as might have been expected, in an acceptance of the Frewins' offer; in a few days Donovan was established in Drury Lane, and with all the natural force of his character, and the retaliatory spirit produced by Ellis's injustice, and fostered by Noir's sympathy, had plunged into the lowest and most painful phase of his life.

Poor old Rouge Frewin was the only gainer by the new arrangement. He had always disliked the part his son had made him play, and to be left at home in peace with his parrot and his pipe, and as much cognac as he could manage to get hold of, seemed to him all that heart could wish. He took the most vehement liking to Donovan, and, in his odd way, was very kind to him; the secret of his affection probably lay in this: the new-comer treated him with respect, and the poor old captain was now so little used to such treatment, that it was doubly delightful to him.

"I am a better fellow since you came," he would often say, looking up with real affection in his little watery eyes at the dark handsome face of his boy-friend—the face which seemed to grow harder, yet more hopelessly sad every day.

It was a world of nicknames into which Donovan had fallen; in the club to which he and the Frewins belonged—a club which was a gaming-house in everything but the prohibited name—every member had been dubbed with some *sobriquet*, often of singular appropriateness. Noir's Dartmoor friend for instance was familiarly known as Darky Legge. The two Frewins had received their names of Rouge et Noir, and before very long Donovan, whether he liked it or not, was invariably addressed as "Milord." The parrot was the first to draw his attention to it, but certainly old Rouge must have taught him, for when ever Donovan came into the room, or attracted the bird's notice in any way, Sweepstakes would scream out "Well, milord! Well, milord!" in his harsh voice, often adding remarks which were quite the reverse of complimentary.

One morning, while Donovan was sitting in the little parlour with a cigar and a newspaper, circumstances combined together in such a way as to make him for the first time ashamed of himself. They had been out very late on the previous night, or rather that morning, and Noir was lying half asleep on the sofa; as the clock struck twelve, however, he roused himself, and with many yawns and stretches prepared to go out.

"Look here, milord," he said, turning at the door, "I've an appointment in the City, and must be off. You'll remember that we've arranged to go down to Manchester by the evening express; be in the way about that time, and I'll join you here on the way to Euston."

"All right," said Donovan, not looking up.

"Yes, but be sure you remember, for I've reason to believe we shall make a good thing of it. Do you hear?"

"Yes," replied Donovan, shortly.

"What on earth makes you such a sulky

brute to-day? One would have thought the luck had been against you instead of all on your side last night," said Noir, glancing at him rather curiously. His question met with no reply, however, and with a shrug of the shoulders he turned away.

When the door had closed behind him, Donovan threw down his paper, and sat silently thinking over the words which had stirred long dormant feelings in his heart. How he disliked this arranging and scheming!—what paltry work he was engaged in!—how low and base and despicable it all was! There was much to dislike, too, in Noir Frewin; in spite of his misfortunes, and the consequent sympathy which had arisen between them, there was necessarily a great deal in him which was most repulsive to Donovan. Old Rouge, moreover, had managed to escape his son's vigilance, and had made a disgraceful scene on the previous evening. Altogether, Donovan felt disappointed with his companions and disgusted with his work—not yet, unfortunately, with himself.

He could not help feeling sorry, however, for Rouge when the old man came slowly and wearily into the room; remembering how his intemperance had begun, and what a good-hearted old fellow he was, his contempt and utter disgust, which had been strongly roused the previous night, died away into pity.

"Good morning, captain," he said, in his usual voice, and using the title which he knew the old man liked better than anything.

"Eh, Donovan, my lad, it's anything but a good morning," sighed poor Rouge, stretching himself out on the sofa. "How one does pay for a little extra enjoyment!" Then, catching a look of contempt on his companion's face, he added, piteously, "Don't you turn against me, lad; I know I'm not what I should be, but don't you give me up too; everyone despises me now, everyone looks down on me, and thinks anything good enough for such a poor old fool. Don't you take to it too, lad, for you've been good to the old captain till now."

"I don't wish to change," said Donovan, "but I hope you won't repeat last night's amusement. How can you expect anyone to respect you, when—well, after all, it's no business of mine."

Rouge sighed heavily.

"Such is life!" screamed the parrot, mimicking the sigh.

Then there was silence in the room for a few

minutes, till the old man broke forth again, this time with the tears running down his cheeks.

"I'm a miserable old sinner, there's no doubt of that, but I was driven to it. It's easy for other people to talk who don't know what temptation is, but I tell you, lad, I was driven to it. I was lonely and miserable, and there was more money than I knew what to do with —how could I help it?"

Donovan did not answer; he crossed the room, and leant with his back against the mantelpiece, thinking—thinking more worthy thoughts than usual, too, for his face had something of the old bright look upon it, which nothing had been able to awake since Dot's death. He liked this poor old man genuinely; he liked very few people in the world, but where his love was once given it was very true and sterling—no mere idle pretence, not a selfish taking of what can be got, but a real outgoing from self. Given an object to spend his love upon, he was capable of immense self-sacrifice; it was his bitter misanthropy, and his resolute shutting out of the source of love, which had so cramped and narrowed his life. In spite of all his shortcomings, there was much that was noble in his character; his face was full of eager desire as he turned to the old man—the lofty, almost passionate desire which must come at times to those who have, if it be but one spark of the Divine fire, the longing to turn from evil those who are overwhelmed by it, to save the weak from temptation.

"Captain," he began, dropping the severe, yet half contemptuous tone which he had at first adopted towards the poor old drunkard. "Captain, I know you had hard times, and have a great deal of excuse; but things are different now, and it's your turn to drive back along the road you were driven. Look, we'll have a try together; you give up the drink, for a time at any rate, and so will I."

"Bless my heart!" exclaimed the old captain, starting up. "Why, my dear fellow, I should be dead in a month. Do you think, after all these years, I could give it up in a moment? Why, it's meat and drink to me; I couldn't live without it, I tell you."

"More die by drinking than by abstaining," said Donovan. "I daresay you'd miss it at first, but you'd soon get over it. You couldn't be more miserable than you are this morning after your last night's carouse."

"But to turn teetotaler!" exclaimed Rouge.

"Why, milord, you'd never hear the last of it at the club; we should be the laughing-stock of the place."

"And do you think that you were not their laughing-stock last night?" said Donovan. "Better be laughed at as a teetotaler than as a drunkard. Plain-speaking, you will say, captain; but you and I don't generally mince matters. Come, agree to my bargain, and my respect for you will rise ten degrees."

"You don't think it would kill me, then?" hesitated Rouge.

"Stuff! more likely to add ten years to your life," said Donovan. "Come, now, we'll each sign an agreement to give it up for—say three months."

"So long," groaned poor Rouge. "Think of the dulness! Why, what will life be worth?"

"Not much, indeed," said Donovan, "but more than your present life, at any rate."

And then, after a little more discussion and hesitation, the papers were signed.

By-and-by the old captain fell asleep on the sofa, and Donovan went out to get his lunch, and to test the desirability of water-drinking. In the afternoon he for the first time made his way to the park, with a sort of desire to see the side of the world from which he had been ejected, the gay fashionable world in which only a year before he had moved. Lighting a cigar, he sat down on one of the benches, and scanned the faces of the passing crowd, wondering whether he should see any of his old acquaintance, longing, though he would hardly admit it to himself, for a sight of his mother. Before he had been seated many minutes, a rather prim-looking lady and a bright-faced girl passed by, hesitated a moment, and then took the vacant places on the bench beside him.

"We have still half an hour before the appointment; do let us sit here—it is such fun to watch the people." It was a clear girlish voice which said this, and Donovan involuntarily looked round at the speaker, a little curious to see who it was who could find pleasure in what to him was so full of bitterness.

A fair, rounded face, sunny hair, and well-opened blue-grey eyes. Where had he seen her before? Somewhere, surely, for he remembered the face distinctly now. It was one he had watched and admired—and he admired very few women. He must have heard her speak too, for he recognised her rather unusual voice—a voice in every way suited to the face, mellow and full of tone, with a great gaiety and happiness ringing in it, softening off tenderly now and then into earnestness. He had met dozens of girls last season, but somehow she did not seem like a London girl; she was too fresh and simple. Where could he have seen her?

He listened with a good deal of interest to all she said, though it was nothing in the least remarkable, merely comments on the passers-by, and a laughing defence of fashionable people, when her companion complained of the frivolity and uselessness of their lives.

"Now, auntie, I shall think it is because you and I are on foot and the grand people are driving that you find fault with them; don't you remember the French proverb about the pedestrians commenting on the carriage people?"

"My dear, I should be very sorry to change places with them," answered the prim-looking lady.

"Yes, auntie, you would, I daresay, but really some people just complain of rich people because they envy them, I'm quite sure they do."

This was rather a home-thrust to Donovan, he threw away his cigar, and listened more attentively, but the conversation drifted away to other things, home matters evidently, details and allusions which came very strangely to him in his semi-vagrant life—the last letters there had been from Dick—Nesta's quickness in reading—how father and mother meant to come up to town before they left. He listened to it all half sadly, half amusedly, it was a glimpse of such a different life from his own, such a simple, innocent, pure life, with such strangely different interests! An unaffected girl, sweet, and bright, and pure-minded, how black his life seemed in contrast with hers! Musing on this he lost the thread of their conversation, and as they rose to go he only caught the words, " Yes, I know he doesn't profess much, but he's such a good man, the sort of man one can trust."

A man one can *trust!* how she leant on that last word! and with what a sharp thrill it pierced Donovan's ear. What would she have said of him had she known the sort of work he was engaged upon? He was quite glad she had moved away, for he did not feel fit to be near her. He had disliked Noir Frewin's plan in the morning, now he shrank from it doubly, in the brief revelation of purity, something of his own true character had been brought to the light, he began to see very faintly indeed, but still to see in some degree his own falseness and blackness.

He would not go with Noir that evening; it would involve some trouble, no doubt, if he did not keep his appointment, Noir would be exceedingly vexed, there would inevitably be a quarrel when he returned from Manchester, and of course he would lose the opportunity of enriching himself, but he would not go, with the light of those clear grey eyes fresh in his memory he felt that he really could not.

Scarcely had he made this resolution when he caught sight of his mother's victoria; there was Ellis Farrant looking just as usual, and beside him was Mrs. Farrant. She was leaning back in the carriage so that Donovan only saw her face for an instant, but he fancied that she looked a little paler than usual, a little sad and worried. The sight moved him not a little, he felt a great longing to see her again, and in the evening, not caring to return to Drury Lane, or to go to the club he was in the habit of frequenting, for fear of meeting the Frewins, he turned instead in the direction of Connaught Square. There was the house he knew so well, the house which ought to have been his, with its balconies gay with flowers, and a brougham standing before the door. His mother was probably going out, he would wait and see her as she came down the steps, but he would not himself be seen, that would be too humiliating, he would wait a little way off, and crossing the road, he leant with his back against the square railings. It was a strange watch; bitter feelings mingled with the returning family love as he stood there in the summer twilight; it *was* hard, even his most stern condemner would have been forced to allow that! He was standing alone in the street, cast off by those who should have helped him, watching their comfort and luxury from his state of misery and conscious sin. Instinctively he took up poor Rouge's cry, "He has driven me to it—how can I help going to the dogs, it is his fault!"

And then the house door opened, and one of the footmen came out to the carriage. Donovan watched eagerly, and his breath came fast and hard. There was his mother, quite placid and happy-looking now, with a white Chuddah over her shoulders, and a diamond star in her hair, and there was Ellis, with his opera hat, and his false smiling face, and his shallow politeness.

Certainly, judging by the outward appearance, there could have been no question which was the more to be pitied, the rich man stepping into his carriage, or the unjustly used outcast who looked on in writhing bitterness of soul; but in reality Donovan's misery was as nothing compared with his step-father's. Years of plotting and scheming, years of growing deterioration, harassing anxiety, and patient waiting, all this had Ellis gone through, and for what? For a rich wife, a town house, and a country house, accompanied by an ever-present remorse, a nameless terror of discovery, a wretched sense of shame, and a haunting dread of his victim Donovan. The good was striving within him, it would not abandon him, would not for a moment let him enjoy his unjust gains; he fought against it with all his strength, and tried to be careless and comfortable, but he fought in vain.

They went to the opera that evening and heard "Faust"; it stung him as no sermon would have done. How like his part had been to that of Mephistopheles! how deliberately he had planned his step-son's harm! And above the voices of singers and chorus, above the grand orchestral accompaniment, there rang in his ears one sharp despairing sentence, "Remember how you have goaded me on to ruin!"

Faust and Margherita were nothing to him. He hardly noticed the beautiful little *prima donna*. It was the grim basso, with his red livery, his stealthy yet rapid movements, his satanic look of triumphant cunning, who preached to him that night, as no clergyman in surplice and stole, or gown and Geneva bands, had ever preached to him. In the "serenata," where Mephistopheles sings his mocking song of triumph to the guitar, and augurs further successes for himself, Ellis sat actually shuddering at the horrible sense of likeness. The song was encored. He could bear it no longer, but shrank back into the very furthest corner of the box, trying not to see or hear. By-and-by it was all over, and Ellis, with a grey face, forced up a smile, and tried to talk in his ordinary way, as he led his wife to the carriage. But the effort was intolerable; he was, in truth, a miserable man that night, but happier had he known it for that very misery. It was the sign of that other Presence within him which will not leave us to an unequal struggle with evil.

Donovan, seeing only the prosperous, outward show, knowing nothing of all the real remorse, watched the carriage drive off with feelings which in their vehemence are quite indescribable. He was almost terrified himself at the storm of hatred, and anger, and wild longing for revenge that took possession of his heart, as well he might be, owning nothing to quell it but the power of his own will. He stood quite still, his face pale and rigid with that terrible white-hot passion, the overmastering passion in which great crimes are often committed. In his madness nothing was too dark for him to contemplate, no revenge too sharp to be resolved upon. He had grasped hold of the iron railing of the garden, involuntarily turning away his face from the houses. A voice close to his ear made him start. If the good still strove with Ellis Farrant, still more did it lead Donovan, who was more sinned against than sinning, and to him no fiend like Mephistopheles came to scare and terrify, but a little child was sent to lead him.

"Do you want to come in? I thought I saw you tugging so at the gate, and I came to ask you."

A little girl of nine or ten was addressing him, looking shyly through the iron bars of the gate. No child had spoken to him since Dot had died. This seemed to him like a voice from the grave, and instinctively, even at the remembrance of the love which he deemed all a thing of the past, lost to him for ever, the evil thoughts and the revengeful anger died out of his heart.

"I should like to come in," he said, in reply to the question, "but I have no key."

"I will ask the Fräulein to open the gate," said the little girl, and she ran across the garden, returning in a few minutes with a German lady, who looked up from her knitting rather curiously to see this gentleman who was waiting for admittance. It was easily explained. He had not a key, but he pointed to his mother's house in the square. The Fräulein, without any demur, unlocked the gate and admitted him.

He had not often been into the garden before, but two or three times he had brought Dot there in her invalid chair, and the place was therefore sacred to him. He went at once to her favourite seat, and there, in the cool of the summer evening, better thoughts returned to him. It had been a hot day. The children were all enjoying the change; they had the garden almost to themselves, and, as they played, their laughter and chatter floated to him. It was what he wanted; something innocent, and pure, and merry. A faint, very faint return of little Dot's influence came back to him, and when he left the garden again he was a better man.

Drury Lane had never seemed to him so dingy as when he returned to it that evening. A street-organ was playing a popular air in one part, and a crowd of wretched-looking bareheaded girls were dancing on the pavement. Every now and then he passed one of those appalling courts or alleys which open into the lane, and, pausing once or twice, he caught a glimpse of the seething human crowd, the filth and misery which they lived in; then on again past the shabby gaslit shops, the disreputable-looking passengers, until he almost fell over a little child who ought to have been in bed long before, but who was sitting on the curb-stone, grubbing with both hands in a heap of mud in the gutter. Donovan was very tender over little children. He stooped down at once to see whether he had hurt the small elf. A pair of dancing blue eyes looked up at him from a dirty little face, and something very unsavoury was held towards him, while, with the confidence of a great discoverer, the elf shouted, gleefully,

"See what I've got! A real old duck's foot! A real old duck's foot!"

It was a very pitiful sight, but it touched Donovan; he dropped a penny into the hand which was not occupied with the new treasure and went away moralizing, till, reaching the print-shop, he drew out his key and went up the stairs to the deserted rooms, for even Rouge was gone, and, for the next three days, Donovan was left to the tender mercies of Waif and Sweepstakes.

He lit the gas and took up a book, but the bird awaking caught sight of him, and instantly began in his most scolding tones,

"*Well*, milord, *ain't* you a fool! Oh, lor, *ain't* you a fool!"

Evidently the Frewins had not made any complimentary remarks upon his absence, and doubtless poor Rouge had hardly been fit for the journey. But he could not help it; if he had not seen that bright-faced girl, and been so shamed by her unconscious words, it would have been different. What a strange glimpse of another kind of life she had given him!

Sweepstakes sat with his shrewd grey head on one side, and his crimson tail feathers drooped; before long, with a wicked look in his round eyes, he began to say plaintively,

> "Be yit t'ever so wumble,
> There's no place li k'ome."

"Be quiet," said Donovan, sharply, for the words did not at all suit his present frame of mind.

But Sweepstakes only reiterated,

> "Be yit t'ever so wumble,
> There's no place like—"

Donovan made a dash at the cage with a cloth and interrupted the song, a proceeding which enraged the parrot.

"You go to Tophet!" he screamed, angrily, and then, being out of temper, he swore for five minutes on end, till, for the sake of peace, Donovan had to make up the quarrel.

But there was a good deal of obstinacy about Sweepstakes, and, though he allowed his anger to be appeased by a Brazil nut, he treated Donovan for the rest of the evening to a mild muttered refrain of "Be yit ever so wumble, umble, umble——" *ad infinitum.*

For the first time since he had been in London, Donovan that night went to his room early; he had got into the habit of turning night into day. But he was dull that evening and tired, and it was not much after half-past eleven when he left Sweepstakes for the night and turned into his own shabby little room at the back. A dreary lodging-house bed-room it was, with a strip or two of carpet thrown down over the dirty unscrubbed floor, a mouldering green wall-paper, and over the fireplace one solitary picture in a gilt frame black with age, a dingy sea-piece in oils, a ship being dashed to pieces on rocks. A room is said to show in a certain fashion the character of its occupant; there were only four things here which could in any way bear traces of Donovan's individuality. On the mantelpiece was Dot's cathedral clock, in one corner a great bath, on the chest of drawers one or two anti-theological books by Luke Raeburn, and at the foot of the bed a woolly rug for Waif.

The window was open; it looked out on to that fearful net-work of byeways and alleys which Donovan had seen as he came home. He had often seen them before, but one can see many times and yet never observe. He had generally gone to his room between three and four in the morning when all was quiet enough; this evening it was just after closing time; the public-houses had let loose their wretched throng, and the cry of the city went up to heaven. People talk of the noise of London, and think generally of the street traffic, the crowded pavements, and the ceaseless wheels, but let them once hear the appalling noise of human life in a poor quarter, and they will not complain of anything else. Wild, drunken singing, fierce quarrels, blows, cursing, a Babel of tongues, a wailing of children, angry disputes between men and women, in which too often the woman's voice in its awful harshness seems unlike that of a human creature. These are the sounds one may hear, the fearful realities which make up the dark side of the world's metropolis.

Donovan stood beside the open window and let all this tide of human wretchedness beat upon his ear. He was shocked and awed, struck with a great pity and indignation, for he was not hard-hearted, only narrow-hearted, and though this crampedness kept him from action it did not prevent the great suffering of humanity from touching him with a sense of pity. The incomprehensible suffering! what a mystery it was! it made him wretched and pitiful, and yet angry, though where the fault of all lay he could not have said. Christianity, or rather the horribly false notions of Christianity which he had received, would have said that all these drunkards and degraded beings were forging the chains which should bind them for ever and ever in hell; according to Mrs. Doery's ideas the West End must have seemed the region of the elect, and Drury Lane the abode of that other numerous band who were foredoomed to everlasting torture. Perhaps almost naturally Donovan had a fellow feeling for sinners, for in his very young days, when he had for a short time believed in what he was taught, he had fully made up his mind that Doery was one of the elect, and that he had better go to the other place; now from his atheism, with which he persuaded himself he was quite contented, he looked back with pity, and yet with a little amusement, on the picture of his sturdy defiant childhood, which preferred even the awfully described fiery furnaces to companionship with Doery in an unjust and partial favour.

He turned away from the window at last, but not till he had closed it and drawn down the blind; he shut out the misery of his fellows as he shut out many other things, for at present he was one of those who as Coleridge puts it—

"Sigh for wretchedness, yet shun the wretched."

It was not to be expected that the passing words of a stranger would be sufficient to alter the whole current of Donovan's life, nor did Gladys Tremain exercise such an unheard of influence. The Frewins returned, and after sundry upbraidings from Rouge and a sharp quarrel with Noir, things fell back again to their former state.

Once, quite unexpectedly, he met the grey-eyed stranger again, two or three weeks after their encounter in the park. It was a July evening, the Frewins, Legge, Donovan, and two or three other men were travelling up together from Goodwood. The train was crowded; Mrs. Causton and Gladys, who had been spending the day with some friends, were waiting on the platform of a station not far from Chichester, but they found it almost impossible to get places.

"Such a dreadful crowd, and such disagreeable-looking people," said poor Mrs. Causton, nervously, "what is the reason of it?"

"Goodwood races, mum," said the porter, wondering at her ignorance, "there's room for one in here, and one next door; come, miss, the train's just starting."

"My dear! you can't go alone in there," said Mrs. Causton, distractedly, looking at the not too reputable travellers, but the next carriage was every bit as bad, the train began to move, there was really no help for it, whether she liked it or not, Gladys was shut in alone among this strange-looking crew. She knew there was nothing to fear, but at the same time it was a very uncomfortable predicament, a fast girl would have been amused by such a novel adventure, but Gladys was not fast, she was a pure womanly woman, and though she could not have explained why, she had a peculiar shrinking from these people. The little conversation at the door too had attracted the notice of a coarse-looking man who was sitting next her; he turned round upon her with a cool inquisitive stare, and then made some remark to his neighbour on the other side which caused a general laugh, and Gladys, though she would not have understood a word even had she heard, felt the colour flame up in her cheeks.

"Why can't you behave decently?" said a voice from the other side of the carriage.

"Rouge, it's your deal."

Then Gladys, who had instinctively lowered her eyes, looked up, for the attention of the passengers was diverted from her; with an overcoat spread over their knees, by way of a table, they were soon absorbed in a game of "Nap." She looked round at their faces with a sort of longing to find one from which she need not shrink; all seemed bad, or coarse, or in some way repulsive; exactly opposite her was an elderly man fast asleep, next to him was the one who had called his companions to order. Gladys looked at his face half hopefully, the voice had at least been refined, and the words—well, the best she had heard in this company. The face too was not otherwise than refined, the features were strikingly handsome, there were no tokens of excess about the clear dark complexion, but oh! what a hard bitter saturnine look there was about the whole; he was evidently much younger than any of his companions, yet not one of them looked so reckless and hardened, still she felt that he was a gentleman, and was at once less uncomfortable and forlorn; apparently he took not the slightest notice of her, and that was pleasant after the uncomfortable rude staring and comments.

It was a very strange and very sad revelation to her—a side of life which she had heard of indeed, but had never in the least realised; the temptations of the world, the flesh, and the devil had never shaped themselves in her thoughts into anything half so terrible as this. She had felt impatient when Mrs. Causton had lamented the temptations of London life for Stephen, yet the danger was no imaginary one, for here was one who could not be older than Stephen or Dick surrounded by evil companions, gambling with a recklessness and *sang froid* which bespoke long habit. There was a sort of horrible fascination in it all, she could not help watching the eager faces; on all of them was written the strong desire of gain, on all, except that one dark saturnine face opposite her, which, though apparently caring for little else but the game, never seemed to unbend, in spite of repeated successes. Gladys watched him as he pocketed his winnings, watched pityingly his unmoved face, and once he looked up and their eyes met. It was not a look from which she need shrink; the eyes were not bad eyes—they were very strange, hungry-looking, sad ones. She understood then why he was so different from his companions—evidently in his heart he disliked the life he was leading. By-and-by a dispute arose, a fierce, loud altercation between her disagreeable neighbour and one of the other men; language such as she had never heard was shouted across the carriage, the lookers-on laughed. Poor Gladys glanced across in despair to the one passenger in whom she had any faith; he was leaning back with a look of ineffable disgust and weariness on his handsome face, but, as the angry Babel grew louder, he turned to Gladys; she hardly knew whether she were relieved or only more frightened when he bent forward to speak to her.

"This must be very unpleasant for you," he said, and she knew at once from his manner that she had found a protector. "We shall be at a station in a minute or two, and then, if you like, I will offer to change places with the lady you are with."

"Oh! thank you so much," said Gladys, her frightened eyes brightening with gratitude and relief. "My aunt is in the next carriage, if you really wouldn't mind——"

"Not in the least; I wish I had thought of it before, that you might have been saved this unpleasantness."

Then, without another word, he returned to his former position, but with a less hard and contemptuous expression than before. The others appealed to him for his opinion in the matter of the dispute, and he spoke coldly and quietly, but evidently what he said was to the point; the disputants quieted down, and agreed to some sort of compromise. At last, to Gladys' intense relief, they reached the station. Donovan got up and let down the window, then, looking back, said carelessly,

"You can leave me out in the next deal; I'm going to change carriages."

The announcement caused a chorus of inquiry.

"What's up with milord now?" asked Gladys' neighbour.

"Oh! some craze, I suppose," said a dark-browed man on the other side of the carriage; "he took a moral fit the other night, and rushed away no one knew where. There's no reckoning on him—'a wilful man must have his'—— Why, what's this?" as Donovan returned to help Mrs. Causton in. "We didn't reckon on this, at any rate. Donovan, what *are* you thinking of?"

"A cigar in peace next door," he replied readily; and then he retreated, leaving Gladys greatly relieved, and the card-players not a little embarrassed by the large bundle of tracts which Mrs. Causton began to distribute among them. At London Bridge they saw him again for a minute, and Mrs. Causton pressed two tracts into his hand and thanked him for his courtesy. Gladys looked up at him shyly and gratefully, but did not speak again, except, as he raised his hat and turned away, to utter one earnest-toned "good-bye." He heard it, and treasured it up in his heart—a wish, he knew it was, no mere formal parting, but the wish of a pure-minded woman that good might be with him.

Gladys watched sadly as Noir Frewin rejoined her protector; he was thoroughly out of temper, as she had seen on the journey, and greeted his companion with a torrent of angry reproaches. Gladys caught only a word or two here and there—"Confounded folly!—playing fast and loose with the agreement!"—and one bitter taunt—"A pretty knight-errant to help distressed ladies, such as *you*, a professional——"

But the word gambler did not reach Gladys. She did not then learn what a life Donovan was leading, but she had seen and heard quite enough to know that he was in great need of help, and from that night he always had a place in her prayers. Without that how could she have borne the revelation of evil and wretchedness, the contrast between the shielded life of those she knew, and the life of constant temptation of these her fellow-creatures. Painful as the evening's experience had been, she could not altogether regret it. In after-life she thanked God for that brief journey, upon which had hinged so much.

CHAPTER III.

"THE RAVEN FOR A GUIDE."

What thou wouldst highly
That wouldst thou holily; wouldst not play false,
And yet wouldst wrongly win.
Macbeth.

Till life is coming back, our death we do not feel,
Light must be entering in, our darkness to reveal.
Archbishop Trench.

AS the autumn wore on, both the dog and his master began to show traces of the life they were living. Poor Waif pined for the country. He had always been his master's companion in his long rides and walks, and town life was of course a great and very undesirable change for him. Donovan, too, lost his strength considerably. It was an unhealthy life he was leading, full of the worst kind of excitement; at times idle and unoccupied, at times full of fatigue. Naturally, too, his state of mind told on his physical strength. The year beginning with the terrible strain of little Dot's death, had brought him overwhelming grief; the long spring months had been spent in a fierce inward struggle, a vain search for peace; then had followed his quarrel with Ellis and his expulsion from Oakdene, and ever since that he had been in the poisoned atmosphere of the society into which Noir Frewin had led him. No wonder that as the winter advanced he began to fail; even the Frewins, who were not more observant of such trivial matters than selfish people usually are, noticed at last that something was wrong.

"There's no getting a rise out of the boy now," observed Rouge, one December afternoon. "I don't know what's come to him, unless, as I expect, it's this absurd fad he's taken into his head about water-drinking. I told him it was enough to kill a fellow to give it up all at once like that. I should have died that very week, if I'd kept my agreement."

Noir gave a contemptuous sneer.

"No fear of your dying in that way, at any rate. I wonder Donovan was ever such a fool as to think you'd give it up. He is an odd fish. There's no making him out."

Rouge glanced at the subject of all this talk, who was lying asleep on the sofa, and then for the first time he noticed how worn and thin he was. All the boyishness had gone from his face now.

"I say, Noir, he looks to me uncommonly queer," said the old captain. "I've seen one or two fellows look like that before now. There was one, I remember, on the *Metora*."

"Pooh! I daresay many of them looked badly enough before they'd found their sea-legs," said Noir, coolly.

"Well, the fellow I mean died," said the captain, impressively. "And I must say milord does look to me awfully out of health."

"Oh! nonsense. He's only seedy—a cold, or something of that sort. We got drenched the other night coming from Legge's place. It's time we were starting. Just wake him up."

Rouge complied, and Donovan started up at once, and looked sleepily at his watch.

"Time to go? Oh! I'd forgotten. It's this Brighton scheme."

He looked wretchedly ill and tired, not at all fit to turn out of the warm room into the cold drizzle of the December twilight, but he was not one to shirk an engagement for the sake of mere bodily disinclination, and there was no one to tell him what madness it was to trifle with such a severe chill as he had taken. He drew on his great-coat, and without a word stood waiting for Noir, who was sorting his cards on a side-table.

"Take my advice," said Rouge, paternally, "and have something just to hearten you up before you go. With such a cold you want something to warm the cockles of your heart."

For the moment Donovan was strongly tempted. He did feel very much in need of some such comfort, but his hesitation was but momentary. He knew that his only hope of influencing the old captain lay in the steadiest adherence to his plan of abstinence. The three months of the agreement were over, but, though Rouge had long ago broken his pledge, his companion's example had often kept him from excess, and Donovan knew well enough that even for his own sake the safe-guard was a very good thing.

"Oh! as to the cockles of one's heart," he said, laughing, "that's all bosh; one only takes cold the easier, as any doctor would tell you. Present loss, future gain, is our motto to-day; we ought to bag a good many head of game to make up for turning out in this wet mist. Good-bye, captain; look after Waif."

And then Noir and his young accomplice set out on their expedition. As they passed the window of the print-shop, Donovan involuntarily paused.

"Why, there's your very double," he said, laughing; and, in spite of the rain, Noir stopped to see what he meant.

It was an old print of Brunel the engineer. The curious forehead and eyebrows, and the general cast of countenance, certainly bore a strong resemblance to Noir, though the expression was very different. Underneath, in copper-plate, was written the couplet—

"Whose public works will best attest his fame,
Whilst private worth adds value to his name."

It was rather a curious contrast to Noir Frewin's life, and the words stung him.

"Well, well!" he said, with his bitter laugh, "my 'public works' are not of the first water, perhaps; you needn't give me that epitaph."

The Brighton expedition proved a great success. Noir and Donovan returned in two or three days' time well content. They had chosen an evening train to come back by. Noir went on as usual to select a favourable carriage; Donovan followed him more leisurely, for it answered their purpose best not to appear to be companions. Donovan's part was usually that of a decoy, a well-to-do, gentlemanly-looking fellow who consented to play, and thus induced others to try their hand. Noir had this evening chosen a most auspicious-looking carriage full of young men returning to town, for it was the week after Christmas, and, the brief holiday being over, many had chosen this late train to take them back to the busy London life again. Scarcely had they left the station, however, when Noir's countenance suddenly fell; two or three of the passengers were commenting on a placard which, printed in large letters, was put up on the side of the carriage. He was vexed and disconcerted, for it effectually put an end to his schemes for the journey. With a slight warning pressure on his companion's foot, he drew his attention to the placard which was above his head. Not in the least knowing what to expect, Donovan took off his hat and put it in the netting, thus getting an opportunity of turning round, and there, staring at him in large type, were words which he never forgot, words which seemed to burn themselves in upon his brain at the very first reading. "Caution. Passengers are earnestly recommended to beware of pickpockets and card-sharpers dressed as gentlemen," &c, &c. He could read no further; he fell back into his place like one stunned, then the hot colour rushed to his cheeks, mounted higher and higher till his whole face seemed to burn and tingle. Had he actually come to this? Was he, Donovan Farrant, a cheat against whom the public must be warned, classed with pickpockets? He, his father's only son, had sunk so low then, that this description would apply to him—a "card-sharper dressed as a gentleman!" That moment's sharp realisation was terrible. Noir, anxious to veil his sudden confusion, held out a newspaper to him; but he only shook his head, and the elder man, who was merely annoyed by the occurrence, began to feel alarmed at the strange effect the caution had had on his accomplice. Such misery, such shame, were written on his face that Noir began to fear he should lose his able assistance.

They got out at London Bridge, and he linked his arm within Donovan's with an anxious attempt at raillery.

"Why, milord, what made you play such a false card just now, colouring up like a girl at a mere piece of paper? I gave you credit for more self-control."

Donovan bit his lip; the last words vexed him, and changed the current of his thoughts, for he rather prided himself on his powers of self-control, which were indeed considerable.

"It startled me," he confessed, after a brief silence. Then again, with a slight hesitation, "Noir, do you consider yourself a card-sharper?"

The question was asked with a kind of innocence which made Noir shudder; he forced up a mocking laugh, however.

"Ask a thief if he considers himself a thief, and he will tell you 'no,' but a professional adept, with a gift for acquiring other people's property."

Donovan winced.

"If that's the definition of a thief, you and I belong pretty much to the same class."

Noir wrenched away his arm.

"And what do I care if we do?" he cried, angrily; "I don't know what makes you so cantankerous to-night. Have you forgotten your favourite maxim, that the world is a mass of injustice, and that a little more or less evil makes no difference? You stand by that, and I'll undertake to stand by you, for the world *is* unjust, and I delight in cheating it when I've the opportunity. If you're going to turn moral, milord, we'll dissolve partnership at once, and you can go back to those fine friends you know, who were so ready to help you before you came to us."

Donovan did not reply to this taunt, he only shivered and drew his comforter over his mouth. He felt worn out and giddy, his steps began to falter, and Noir, who in his strange rough fashion loved him, forgot his anger, and taking his arm again, half dragged him home.

"The fact is, you're seedy and down in the mouth, Donovan," he said, as they reached their rooms, "you'll see things very differently tomorrow."

Donovan did not answer, he stumbled up the dark staircase after Noir, and followed him into the parlour. There, with the gas flaring, a huge fire blazing up the chimney, and supper waiting on the table, was the old captain; his hearty welcome was generally pleasant enough, but this evening Donovan felt he could not stand it. He was half perished with cold and involuntarily made for the fire, but it was only for a minute, the warm comfortable room was not in keeping with his doubt and misery.

"Double, double,
Toil and trouble,"

sang Sweepstakes, following the tall dark figure with his shrewd eye, "Double—double—dou-ble——dou—ble."

"First-rate luck all three days," Noir was saying. "To-night our little game was stopped, and milord's down in the depths. Here, Donovan, come to supper, we didn't get much of a feed at Brighton."

But Donovan shook his head.

"Good night, captain," he said, and, disregarding Rouge's remonstrances, left the room. He opened his own door, and Waif, with whines of delight, sprang to greet him.

"Waif—poor old fellow!" he exclaimed, stooping for a minute over the dog, but hastily raising himself again. "No, no, down, get down, I say, I'm not fit to touch you."

Poor Waif was utterly bewildered, his master had never spoken to him in that way before, something must be wrong, very much wrong. It was dark, but the faintest glimmer of light from the uncurtained window served to show him that his master had thrown himself on the ground, it was a sure sign that he was in trouble, Waif knew that perfectly well, and did not just at first dare to interrupt him; he walked disconsolately round and round him, stopping every minute or two to sniff at him, listen, whine in a subdued way.

Donovan was beyond dog help just then, in the depth of his self-abasement he could not sink low enough, in his abject self-loathing to be touched by a being whom he loved would have been unbearable. He had known well enough that he was doing wrong before. Something of his blackness had been borne in upon him when Gladys Tremain had spoken those words in the Park, but now it was all before him, in hideous array, the very vision of sin itself. How could he have delighted in anything so ghastly? it was not even a great revenge he had taken on the unjust world, but the pettiest, meanest, most despicable revenge. What had he not fallen to in these months? why, these hands of his—the hands that had waited on Dot—had stooped to pick up paltry half-crowns won by cheating foolish wretches in a railway-carriage. And then came the remembrance of his father. "You are hardly in a position, Dono, to speak of breaches of honour." Not even then! oh! what would his father have said to him now! Yet little as he had known of him, that little was enough to tell him that his father would always think more of the future than of the past. There was a future for him even now, he must no longer wage war upon the unjust world, he must—he *would* alter his way of living if only for the sake of redeeming his father's name. But for the first time in his life he felt a want in himself, that agony of remorse, despair, utter self-abhorrence had done its work, he was no longer blindly confident in his own strength.

Presently from sheer exhaustion he fell asleep. Waif was happier when he heard the deep regular breaths; a strange process of thinking began in the dog mind. He went back to his woolly rug and lay down, but in a minute jumped up again, ran to his master, licked his hand, and then returned to his rug. Still he could not settle himself to sleep, a second and a third time he got up, making an uneasy circuit round the prostrate figure on the ground. At last, as if unable to lie on his rug while Donovan was on the floor, he curled himself up at his feet, and there slept peacefully.

In the adjoining room Noir, having made a hearty meal, drew up his chair to the fire and lighted his evening pipe. The old captain was evidently uneasy. Noir was uneasy, too, in reality, but he kept it to himself.

"He's a very queer customer that lad," said Rouge, meditatively. "You think it really is this piece of paper which frightened him?"

"Yes, he's young," said Noir, in an excusing tone. "It gave him a turn, I daresay it will soon pass off. If not we must get a little change somehow. It wouldn't be a bad plan to go abroad for a month or two, plenty to be done there, and he'd be sure to like it. After all, of course we do run some risk here; a month or two of absence wouldn't be a bad notion."

"'He who prigs what isn't his'n,'" quoted Rouge. "Well, don't carry it too far, and don't drive the boy away, whatever you do."

"No, no, I'd sacrifice a good deal to keep him," said Noir, "but he's thoroughly upset to-night about it."

Presently the old captain lighted his candle and went up to bed, but Noir sat on long after his pipe was finished, long after the fire had sunk down in the grate to a handful of dying embers; he was thinking, brooding painfully over the comparative innocence of his boy accomplice, and his own villainy. How despairing and wild the fellow had looked, too, as he left the room; he quite started when the door opened, and Rouge, with his nightcap on, appeared again upon the scene.

"I say, Noir, I don't feel happy about that boy. It was very strange of him to go off like that with no supper."

"Pooh!" said Noir, contemptuously, though his father was speaking his own thoughts. "He's ashamed of himself and vexed about that caution."

"Yes; but to go off ill as he is, cold and supperless. If he was a Catholic he might do it as penance, but he's nothing, you know."

It did not strike them that in very deep inward trouble it is at times impossible to enjoy or permit bodily ease; indeed, if the poor old captain had been guilty of the most heinous crime, he would probably have eaten his supper after its committal, and found a solace in the eating to his pangs of remorse. He could not understand anything which went deeper than this, and his good heart had been stirred with pity as he lay down warmed and satisfied in his comfortable feather-bed.

Noir's thoughts went at once to darker suspicions; he had seen something of that same despairing look on Donovan's face when, on that bright June afternoon, he had watched him unknown on Westminster Bridge. He had read his intentions then, was it possible that misery and shame had driven him again to the same longing?

"We'll just give him a look on our way up," he said, carelessly. And then he turned the door-handle noiselessly, and with well-disguised anxiety stole in; the room was very quiet, the bed empty. Noir's heart stood still, and, with an exclamation of dismay, he hurried to the dark form which was stretched out on the floor.

"Bring the candle quick," he said to his father, and Rouge, trembling with fear, held the light nearer, while Waif growled a little at the unusual disturbance.

Noir bent down for a moment close to the half-hidden face, then he started up again with an expression of relief, which came rather oddly from his lips—

"Thank God!"

"Well, it did give me a turn," said the old captain, stooping to pat the dog.

"Hush!" said Noir, "you'll wake him."

And then for a minute the shabby little room witnessed a strange scene. Donovan stirred uneasily, half turned round, but sank again into profound sleep, and the two Frewins bent over him, why, they could scarcely have said, but in their relief it seemed almost a necessity. They watched the face of the sleeper—flushed as if even now the shame were making itself felt— the sad face which seemed all the more despairing because of its stillness, the fixedness of its misery. And Noir's heart smote him, his conscience cried out loudly, "You have brought him to this, you have dragged this boy down into shame and dishonesty."

Rouge thought only of the discomforts of a night on the floor.

"Wake him up," he urged. "It's frightfully cold, he oughtn't to be there."

But Noir would not wake him, he knew that it would be cruel to bring him back to his anguish of remorse. Rouge could never understand anything higher than bodily comfort, it was what he lived for; his son, though a far worse man, had nevertheless a capability of entering into greater things, he had himself sinned and suffered, and though it was years since he had known real remorse, he had once known it, and to a certain extent he understood Donovan's feelings.

"Better leave him," he said; but, with the words upon his lips, he nevertheless turned to the bed, and, dragging off a railway-rug which covered it, threw it over the prostrate form on the floor. Strangely indeed in life do the lights and shades intermix, faint flickerings of the light divine stealing in, in spite of the vast black shades of sin.

The next day—the last of the year—was a dreary one in the Frewins' rooms. Noir kept out of the way, not caring to face his accomplice; old Rouge, in great depression, dusted his curiosities as usual, and put things tidy and ship-shape; and Donovan sat coughing and shivering over the fire, with an expression of such despondency, often of such terrible suffering, that the old captain scarcely dared to speak to him. The sharpness of his remorse had for the time died away, it was swallowed up in the misery of his recollections, for this was the anniversary of Dot's last day of life, and remembrances strange, tender, pitiful, but always full of pain, thronged up in his mind. Brooding over it all, his brain excited with the events of the past night, his body worn out with pain, it was no wonder that the overtaxed nature at last gave way.

His mood seemed to change; Rouge, who had not been able to extract a word from him all day, was astounded as the evening drew on to find him suddenly in the wildest spirits.

"Come," he said, "we'll go to Olliver's; it's time we had dinner. Come along, captain."

And poor old Rouge found himself dragged off, in spite of his remonstrances.

"You'd better not go out, milord; you're really not fit."

"Not fit!" said Donovan, with a mad laugh, cut short by a cough. "I'm fit for anything. Come along, old fellow; we'll drown care, stifle it, kill it, what you like!"

Rouge, really frightened, panted along after his crazy companion, with difficulty keeping pace with his fevered steps; and then ensued an evening of mad merriment. A year ago, only a year ago, and Donovan had been watching Dot's last agony; with the strong manly tenderness of great love he had held the little quivering hands in his, now in a crowded billiard-room he grasped the cue instead, and betted wildly, losing, winning, winning again considerably, then with the Frewins, and Legge, and two or three other companions returning to Drury Lane and gambling the old year out and the new year in.

"I back the winner, I back the winner!" screamed Sweepstakes from his cage.

And above the sounds of dispute, and merriment, and eager play, the clock of St. Mary's Church struck twelve, and in the distance Big Ben's deep notes echoed over the city, and, just because an agony of remembrance rushed back into Donovan's mind, he staked higher and higher. The room rang with his wild laughter.

Noir broke up the gathering much earlier than usual, and with flushed cheeks and wild glittering eyes Donovan staggered to his feet; but he could hardly stand, his head seemed weighted, his limbs powerless.

"I've done for myself now," he said, catching at Noir to keep himself up. Noir did not answer; with his father's assistance he helped him into the next room, and with some pangs of conscience kept guard over him through the night of mad excitement and misery which followed.

The next morning the bright new year broke over the great city, there were *fêtes*, and rejoicings, and merry family parties, but in the lodging-house in Drury Lane all was silent, even at night no gamblers' wild revelry broke the stillness, for Donovan was prostrated by an attack of congestion of the lungs in its acutest form.

CHAPTER IV.

STRUGGLING ON.

Men are led by strange ways. One should have tolerance for a man, hope of him; leave him to try yet what he will do.
On Heroes and Hero-worship.

May we not again say, that in the huge mass of evil, as it rolls and swells, there is ever some good working imprisoned; working towards deliverance and triumph?
French Revolution. CARLYLE.

HE had known for a long time that he was out of health, and at times the dread of being ill had haunted him painfully, as it will at times haunt those who are practically homeless. For it is indeed very terrible to face the thought of illness with no mother at hand to nurse you, no sister to whom the duties of tending will be a pleasure rather than a tiresome duty, no house in which you have a right to be ill, where you need not feel burdened with the sense of the trouble you are causing. To Donovan, with his utter want of belief in human nature, or in the very existence of anything above human nature, the sense of helplessness came with double power; only, fortunately for him, things were not really as he believed. Close beside him, though unknown, the love of the All-Father watched and shielded from evil the son who, by such wretched wanderings, was being led on. And the pity which springs up very readily in most of our hearts, when we are brought face to face with pain, brought human help and comfort to his sick-bed. The landlady, careworn and harassed with many children and a good-for-nothing husband, yet found time to do the few absolutely necessary things in the sick-room; she could not help being sorry for her apparently friendless lodger. Once or twice she pained him terribly by asking,

"Haven't you no mother who could come and see to you?"

And Donovan would sign a negative, and, when she had left him to himself, would feel the loneliness and suffering with double keenness.

Noir Frewin would come in two or three

times a day and ask how he was; the old captain would hang about the room with anxiety written on his kind old face, but he missed his companion's vigilance and example, the drinking mania seized him strongly, and he was seldom quite sober. There was one other amateur nurse, the poor little over-driven servant. She used to shuffle into the room every now and then, and with infinite care and clumsiness would drag the pillow from under his head, shake it up violently and turn it, or hold a glass to his burning lips and spill half its contents down his night-shirt, but he learnt to be grateful even for such rough attentions, for there is nothing like weakness and suffering for teaching patience. The loneliness was so terrible, too, that he would detain anyone who came to him as long as possible. Old Rouge, with his unsteady gait and half incoherent talk, was better than no one, and even the little slipshod servant, with her rough head and dirty hands, was worth the exertion of talking, just for the sake of having a human creature within reach.

"I allays liked you, sir," she said to him once. "You ain't allays a-calling for your boots, like Mr. Frewin, or in drink, like the captain, and you never shouted out 'slavey' down the stairs for me, as though I was one of the poor blacks. I allays liked you, Mr. Donovan."

Donovan was amused, and in spite of his burning head and aching misery, threw out some question or response to detain her.

"And I've done things for you as I've not done for no other lodger," the girl continued. "I've blacked your boots a sight better than any of the others, and though you did want such a terrible lot of bath water hevery day, I allays brought it up reg'lar. If the lodgers h' is civil and kind-spoken, I do my best for 'em, but most of 'em—why, they treat us poor girls like dogs, that they do. And talkin' of dogs, I've done that un of yours many a good turn; times and times I've stolen bits o' meat and things for 'im."

"Oh! but you shouldn't do that," said Donovan, quickly. "Don't do it again. It's wrong to steal, you know."

But then he paused. What was he saying? How trivial were this poor ignorant girl's dishonesties compared with his own!

Bitter were the regrets which thronged up in his mind as he lay wearily on his bed of pain. He could not escape from his secret foes now;

he could not banish thought by violent bodily exercise, or by wild excitement. All his anguish of last year returned with terrible force, all the agony of self-loathing weighed upon him with cruel ceaselessness. This, combined with the want of good nursing, aggravated his illness. The doctor began to look grave, and one day Anne, the little servant, fairly burst into tears when she came up to tidy his room.

"What's the matter?" asked Donovan, feebly. "Have they been scolding you?"

"No, no, it ain't that," said the girl, holding her apron to her eyes. "But missus she says you'll die, sure as a gun; she did say so, I heared her, sir, not a minute since."

Donovan did not speak for some time. He lay thinking silently over the girl's words, "You'll die, sure as a gun." He smiled a little, thinking that few had been told of their danger in a more open and undisguised way, but it ought to have been good news to him, and for a time he tried to think he was glad. And yet? He did not go straight to the root of the matter, and own that the "peace of nothingness" looked less attractive when viewed nearly; he said instead what a wretched life he had had, how little enjoyment, how much suffering, and now he was to die forlorn and unattended in a miserable London lodging. Then came a great longing to see his mother.

He called the girl to him, made her find writing materials, and, raising himself on his elbow, wrote with great difficulty a few pencil words.

"I am very ill; my death will perhaps ease more consciences than one. Will you not come to me, mother?—it may be our last meeting."

He was growing faint; the effort had been very great, but, still exerting all his strength of will, he controlled his weakness sufficiently to scrawl the address on the envelope. Then he sank back again utterly exhausted.

"You'll have to see the clergyman if you get worse," said Anne, sympathetically. "There's one as come next door to an old chap as was dying last summer, and they say he do make the folks quake and sweat."

Donovan was past smiling.

After that he did not remember much; there was only an ever-present consciousness of endless pain, the raging, burning, aching misery of fever. Till then the hours had dragged on with the terrible slowness of which only those who have been alone in illness can form any idea;

but now he lost all thought of time, and was only dimly aware of the visitors who came to him. Now and then he had a sort of vision of Rouge's round red face anxiously peering down at him. Once he fancied himself chained down in one of Doery's red-hot furnaces, where Dives-like he had cried for water, and then he had looked up, and Noir was beside him with the cooling draught he had thirsted for, and he had fallen back again refreshed, wondering greatly that his request had been granted. The Christian's God was, after all then, merciful! Wild thoughts they were which haunted him in his delirium; and yet Noir Frewin, as he watched beside him, was struck by the tone of his fevered utterances. He was prepared for ravings against injustice, but, instead, Donovan's most vehement words were of self-reproach. At times he would take a theological turn, and would argue for and against every conceivable doctrine, and then again he would fancy himself back among his late companions, gambling or indulging in wild revelry; but throughout there was never one impure word, and Noir marvelled at it. A strange wild life was revealed, with an undercurrent of anxious questioning, one predominant vice, but behind it much that was noble, a familiarity with every kind of evil, but, in spite of it, a strange retaining of purity.

One name, too, was constantly on his lips—a name which Noir had never heard him mention before. He wondered much to whom it referred, what gave rise to the agonised longing for this one presence.

Perhaps in this was Donovan's keenest suffering. He dreamt continually of Dot; she was beside him, no longer ill and helpless, but happy, and strong, and bright. As yet, remembrance was such terrible pain to him—it was so entirely his object not to remember the past—that the vision which kept recurring to him was almost more than he could bear, and the extraordinary reality of it deluded him at times. It must be real, she had come back to him, and he would stretch out his arms to keep her; then, coming to himself, would find that it was only a dream. One night the dream was more vivid than ever. He fancied himself on a wide-open down; he was ill and faint, and the sun was beating down upon him pitilessly. He closed his eyes to shut out the intolerable brightness, and then suddenly became aware of a shade between him and the sun, and, looking up, saw Dot standing beside him. Such a rapturous meeting it was! Her face seemed changed, and yet the same, and her bright eyes shone down upon him with just the old loving light. He could feel her fingers ruffling up his hair as she used to do in the old times, and her voice, merry and child-like as ever, seemed to give him new strength. "It is my turn to nurse you now," she said. And then, just as he was feeling the full bliss of her presence, a thick white mist rose from the ground and rolled between them. He stretched out his hands, tried to struggle up, helplessly beating against the cold white wall. Dot was there just beyond. He must reach her! this sudden meeting, only to part, was too cruel! But the more he dashed himself against the impenetrable barrier, the harder it became, and maddened by hearing her voice in the distance, he grew more and more reckless, till at last his own cry of despair woke him. Trembling, exhausted, panting for breath, he stared round the little room. The scene was changed. Fight as he would, there was no chance of his seeing Dot again; even the white barrier was gone. The gas was turned low, and close beside it sat Noir, nodding over his newspaper. The blank of realisation was so terrible that he felt he *must* call on some one or something outside himself, and his companion was roused by a call so wild, so despairing, that he started up at once and hurried to the bedside.

"What is it?" he questioned, anxiously; but Donovan could not answer; his breath would only come in gasps, his whole frame was convulsed. By the strange freemasonry of suffering, Noir Frewin understood him; he did not say a word, but just took the two burning hands in his, and Donovan, with a sense of relief, tightened his hold till the grip was absolutely painful. Anything human would have served to support him; he clung to the hands of this hardened cheat with helpless gratitude.

And Noir, as he looked down at the struggling agony, understood it all far better than many would have done. A well-regulated mind accustomed to view things quietly, or a Christian who has never known what it is to be anything else, would probably not have known so exactly what to do; they would have offered words to a state utterly beyond the comprehension of speech, or would have advised self-control when the very fact of the convulsed frame and sealed lips showed that no control was needed. But Noir had been through just the same fierce conflicts in his cell at Dartmoor; he knew that no words would avail, no thought comfort, that what nature cried out for was a *presence* stronger than self—something or some one who would not preach, but would understand. He gave, poor fellow, all he could give—himself; and after a time Donovan's convulsed limbs relaxed, the hands loosened their hold, the face settled into its usual stern sad expression.

"Thanks, old fellow," he said, faintly.

Noir, with an odd choking in his throat, turned away and made ready some gruel which had been heating. By the time he had brought it, Donovan had recovered a little more, and there was a sort of smile on his worn face.

"I can't get over you turning nurse, Noir," he said, in rather trembling tones; "you've been—awfully good to me."

"Only make haste and get well," said Noir, roughly, but kindly.

"Am I not doing my best by swallowing this abomination?" said Donovan, trying to form his lips into a smile, but failing piteously.

"You'd better be quiet, or you won't get off to sleep again," said Noir, peremptorily, the fact being that he could not stand the effort at cheerfulness which his patient was making, for there are few things more painful than to see a thin veil of assumed cheerfulness drawn over great suffering. But the effort was a brave one, he could not help knowing it, and as he returned to his place beneath the gas, instead of taking up his newspaper, he mused over the hidden trouble which had been half revealed to him, from time to time casting a glance towards the bed. Nothing, however, was to be seen there except a mass of rough brown hair; Donovan had turned his face away from the light, and Noir only knew that he was not asleep by the absolute stillness of his form, and by the long-drawn but half-restrained sighs which reached him every few minutes.

The next morning the old captain, with his feather-brush, was as usual dusting his shells and corals, when he was interrupted by the little maid-of-all-work.

"If you please, sir," she said, with unusual animation, "'ere's a lady as will 'ave it that Mr. Farrant lives 'ere, and I can't get 'er away no'ow."

Rouge, removing his smoking-cap, hurried forward, and found himself face to face with an elderly woman with a rather thin severe face.

"There must be some mistake, madam," he said, in his pleasant voice. "No one of the name of Farrant lives here. We are the only lodgers, except one poor fellow named Donovan, who is very ill."

"There!" exclaimed Mrs. Doery, with relief. "Now why didn't you tell me that before, though I was certain he must be here somewhere, he'd never make a fault in the address. Take me to him at once, please, sir—I've come to nurse him."

"Bless me!" exclaimed the old captain, "now that's really a wonderful piece of luck, for he's in need of better nursing than we can give him. You are a relation of his?"

"Relation, indeed!" said Mrs. Doery, with virtuous indignation—"relation, sir! A pretty pass he must have come to if you take me for a relation. I am the housekeeper."

"Your pardon, madam," said the captain. "May I not offer you some refreshment after your journey," and he put his hand on the inevitable black bottle which was always within convenient reach.

"I'll thank you, sir, to take me to Mr. Donovan," said Doery, severely, "and not go offering a respectable party spirits at this time of day."

Rouge, feeling snubbed, hastily led the way to the sick-room, muttering under his breath, "A very dragon!" But nevertheless he rather enjoyed the new arrival, and there was a ring of amusement in his hearty voice as he went up to the disordered uncomfortable-looking bed where Donovan lay.

"Well, milord, I've brought you a new nurse."

If anyone had told Donovan in his childhood that he would ever welcome the sight of his grim tyrant he would not have believed it, but nevertheless there was an unspeakable comfort and relief in the advent of poor old Doery.

"Oh! Mr. Donovan, what have they been a-doin' to you?" she exclaimed, horror-struck at his looks, for he was evidently quite clear-headed, but utterly weak and helpless, and with a face so thin and worn that she hardly recognized it.

"Did my mother send you?" he asked, as soon as the captain had left the room.

"No, sir, master sent me, with orders to say nothing about it to mistress. It was the only way he'd let me come, Mr. Donovan, so you mustn't mind. Mistress is to be told I'm gone to nurse my sister. I promised I wouldn't say a word to her, otherwise master wouldn't have told me where you was."

"He opened the letter, then?" asked Donovan.

"He had your letter, sir. I made no doubt it was sent to him, for the mistress hadn't seen it."

Evidently, then, it would be quite useless to attempt writing to his mother; after the lapse of all these months of silence, Ellis still kept guard over her correspondence. A sort of dim idea which had crossed his mind of appealing to his mother for money to start him in some honest calling, died away. He must continue to support himself by his precarious winnings, only—and here all his strength of will asserted itself—he would *never* be a party to Noir's deceptions again. It was not a very cheering prospect, he saw that it must involve an entire break with the Frewins, and they had been so good to him that he shrank very much from the thought. After all, as he often said to himself, his death would solve many difficulties.

But he was not to die—that was evident. Thanks to Mrs. Doery's good nursing he began to recover steadily, and, as his strength returned, a certain enjoyment of life returned to him too, at times. He began to wish very much to be out and about again, even though so many difficulties would have then to be faced.

His intercourse with old Mrs. Doery was a good deal hampered by various causes. He never mentioned Dot's name, he never mentioned his present way of life, so that their range of conversation was rather limited. He asked a thousand questions, indeed, about his mother, and the whole Manor household, but except with regard to this subject he was very silent and utterly uncommunicative. From day to day he would lie with a sort of rigid patience, abstractedly watching Doery as she sat mending his linen, or with his eyes fixed on the hateful little oil-painting of the "Shipwreck," which stared down at him from the dingy green wall paper with black spots. It used to remind him a good deal of his own life, that forlorn-looking vessel with broken mast and battered hull.

One night when he was almost recovered he was roused from his first sleep by noisy merriment in the adjoining room, and found poor Mrs. Doery fairly frightened out of her wits.

"Such a calling and a shouting and a quarrelling as she'd never heard in her life!"

"They are only enjoying themselves," said Donovan, with weary sarcasm.

"Well, Mr. Donovan, it's more like animals than like men, that I will say," replied Doery, with her customary shrewd severity.

"May be," said Donovan, turning from side to side with the restless discomfort of one disturbed.

"And nobody can't deny that it's a dreadful place that you're in," continued the housekeeper. "Such a shocking goings on in them courts out at the back, and then all this noise in the very next room when honest folks ought to be a-bed and asleep. It's a dreadful place, I call it."

"London isn't made up of Connaught Squares," said Donovan, bitterly; and then he drew the bed-clothes over his face, and would not say another word.

The next day was Sunday, and by dint of many assurances of his perfect recovery, Mrs. Doery was at length persuaded to leave him for a little while and go to church, Donovan having over-ruled her dread of losing her way by assuring her that the old captain went every now and then to salve his conscience, and would be delighted to escort her. When she had left him he lay for a few minutes listening to the church bells, but his thoughts were very troublesome that day, and just to stifle them he reached out his hand and took Mrs. Doery's Bible from the table. It was nearly four years since he had opened one, and then it had only been under compulsion at school, and though he had read many books written against it, he had never had the slightest inclination to study the book itself. Beyond a few chapters which he had been made to learn in his childhood as a punishment, he remembered little but the sort of general outline of the history, and a few of the more striking parables.

He took it up now rather curiously, opened at St. Matthew's Gospel, and, skipping the Table of Genealogy, began to read in a careless, cursory way. By-and-by, however, in spite of himself, he grew interested. From the few isolated chapters which he had heard occasionally in church and during his school life, he had never gained any idea of the character of Christ. Now reading straight on, with a great craving after some fresh interest, he was naturally very much struck. A life of poverty, and suffering, and self-denial, a career of apparent failure, surroundings low and incapable of understanding, a trial of glaring injustice, and an unmerited death of the deepest pain! It was a story which could not fail to touch him; a character which filled him with great admiration. There were two things which especially appealed to his sympathy—the injustice suffered, and the strong endurance manifested. He put down the book reluctantly when he was too tired to hold it any longer, not even thinking of any possible change in his fixed beliefs, but simply very much struck by a noble life, which, it seemed probable, had been lived thousands of years ago—with something of the same sort of interest which he had felt for one or two of the old Romans, and for a few of Shakspere's characters. Modern Christianity—or the so-called Christianity which had been brought under his notice—offered no attractions to him. The whole system seemed to him hollow and false, a great profession and a niggardly performance, a mixture of selfishness, hypocrisy, and superstition. But the life of Christ was grand! Such an unexampled career of noble self-devotion filled him with wonder and reverence. However much the misguided followers had fallen off, there could be no doubt that the mind of Christ had been—he naturally used the past tense—one of dazzling purity and beauty.

In the enforced stillness of convalescence the story haunted him strangely, and undoubtedly he was influenced by it—his admiration of a noble mind ennobled him. At present that was all; but it was much.

As soon as he was about again, he took an early oppertunity of telling Noir the decision which he had made before his illness. Noir, who had already shrewdly surmised that he should lose his young accomplice, made no attempt to turn him from his purpose.

"Turned good, I suppose, as most fellows do when they have been within an ace of dying," he remarked, sneeringly.

"Glad to hear you think so," said Donovan, with coolness. "I own you've a proverb to fall back on. 'The Devil he fell sick; the Devil a monk would be.' However, I've no monkish tendencies, only I don't mean to be your decoy any longer."

"Well," said Noir, good-humouredly, "I myself shan't be sorry to leave the old trade for a bit. We've been talking of going abroad. Come with us. It would set you up in no time. What do you say to Monaco? A try at the red and black?"

"Anything for a change," said Donovan; but there was relief in his tone, for the break with the Frewins, which he had dreaded a good deal, would be no longer necessary. " Honest " gambling of course he had not renounced, in fact by means of it he must live, and this proposal to go to Monaco exactly fell in with his present frame of mind. His spirits began to rise.

The old captain coming into the room was surprised at the change in his look and voice.

" Well, captain!" he exclaimed. " Has Noir told you? It's all settled, we leave this hole next week, and go to try our luck at Monte Carlo."

"So I hear," said Rouge. "It'll be first rate for you, for myself I like Old England best. None of your froggy Frenchmen for me. I'm going out, milord, d'you want anything? papers? books?"

A change came over Donovan's face.

"Oh! yes, that reminds me. Here!"—he threw down eighteen pence on the table, scrawled something on a piece of paper and handed it to Rouge,—" Just get me that if you're passing a book-shop."

The captain looked at the paper, lifted his eyebrows, but did not venture any comment. On it was written, " Renan's 'Life of Jesus.'"

CHAPTER V.

MONACO.

I heard a thousand blended notes
While in a grove I sat reclined,
In that sweet mood when pleasant thoughts
Bring sad ones to the mind.

To her fair works did Nature link
The human soul that through me ran ;
And much it grieved my heart to think
What man had made of man.
WORDSWORTH.

Spots of blackness in creation to make its colours felt.
Modern Painters.

"NOW this is first rate," said the old captain, as he stepped off the pier at Folkestone on to the steamer. "Ah, Donovan, my lad, if we were going for a good cruise it would do you all the good in the world, better than a dozen Monacos, eh? Not so profitable, you say? Well, perhaps not, but I wish I was captain of the *Metora* again, a prime little steamer she was, you wouldn't think much of such a tub as this if you'd been aboard the *Metora*."

Donovan, with the delicious sense of returning strength, rolled himself up in his railway-rug, and with his elbow resting on the deck railing looked out seawards. The captain was in great spirits, the breath of sea air seemed to awake his better self, and he was besides very happy in having his favourite companion with him again.

"Now that you're about again, milord, I shall be a different man," he said, cheerily; "I've been dreadfully down in the mouth since you were ill, I missed you frightfully; and there was Noir as grim as death, and even Sweepstakes as cross as could be. You wouldn't believe what a bother we had with that bird, milord; just after you were laid up he caught, somehow or other, one of his old couplets which always enrages Noir. I suppose I'd said it, and he'd remembered it, for day and night that creature said nothing but,

"He who prigs what isn't his'n;"

you know the old rhyme!"

"There's something uncanny about Sweepstakes," said Donovan, laughing, "he has a good deal of the wizard about him. It's to be hoped he'll be quiet on the journey, or Noir will threaten to wring his neck."

"Yes, he doesn't approve of our menagerie," said Rouge, adjusting the covering of the parrot's cage, "though I will say that the dog is a marvel of obedience."

"I back the winner!" screamed Sweepstakes, as the bell sounded and the steamer began to move. "Now be gentle, be gentle."

"Hullo! the creature is beginning to talk," said Donovan, "you'll have a crowd round him."

And true enough before long they found themselves the centre of an amused group, to whom the parrot held forth in his choicest language. But presently Noir came up, and directly the bird caught sight of him he put his head on one side and began with his most sanctimonious manner to say,

> "He who prigs what isn't his'n
> When he's cotched shall go to pris'n."

"You must keep the parrot quiet," said Noir, crossly, "he's disturbing the whole deck."

The passengers at once disclaimed this, and expressed their admiration of the bird's cleverness, but Noir was not to be baffled, he drew the black covering over the cage, and Donovan saw by the frown on his brow that he was vexed by this particular sentence of the malicious parrot. He sat down on the other side of the cage, ready to check any further talking, but he could not prevent the mild refrain which Sweepstakes invariably resorted to when he was snubbed, and all through the crossing he gently murmured to himself, "When he's cotched—cotch—cotch—cotched!"

It was a grey day at the end of February, and the English shore was enveloped in mist, but there was, nevertheless, a strong breeze blowing. "East-nor'-east," Rouge declared it to be, "and a heavy swell which would prove fatal to the land-lubbers."

Donovan, though making no pretensions as to his sailing powers, enjoyed the change and novelty most thoroughly, and, indeed, after seven or eight weeks of the unwholesome atmosphere of Drury Lane, the fresh sea-breeze was almost intoxicating. In spite of adverse circumstances and a naturally melancholy temperament, the young life within him sprang up to greet the novelty of all around, his eyes brightened, his taciturnity disappeared, and he and the old captain sat talking together as happily as two school-boys.

Then came the landing at the sunny little French town, with the chatter of bad English and broken French, the hurry and bustle of the passengers, Rouge's anxiety over his precious parrot, and Donovan's difficulty in steering him safely past the door of the *buffet*, with all its temptations. After a few minutes' delay, they were off once more, fairly started now on their route to the south, and Donovan, in the first exuberance of his new strength, really thought he had found something to satisfy his restlessness, and to fill the emptiness of his life. Fair France, with her sunny plains and genial atmosphere, looked very tempting, Monaco offered plenty of excitement—why should he not be happy now?

They were to travel straight on to Nice, a rash project for a semi-invalid, but naturally the Frewins consulted their own wishes, and Donovan, though tired enough when they reached Paris, preferred going on with them to staying for the night alone, for he was still not at all fit to be left quite to himself; old Mrs. Doery had only resigned her post a few days before, and he shrank from entire self-dependence. So the night journey was undertaken, and he sat back in his corner watching his sleeping companions, sometimes dozing himself for a few minutes, but oftener wide awake, and fully conscious of his weary misery, bearing it with a sort of philosophic endurance, and thinking a good deal of the life he had left behind him, of his parting conversation with Mrs. Doery, of the interview which by this time she had probably had with his step-father, of the luck which he had had at the club a few nights ago, which had enabled him to pay his doctor's bill and start comfortably on his foreign trip, and of sundry passages which had impressed him in Renan's book. An odd medley, truly, in an utterly unregulated but well-disposed mind —well-disposed, that is, as far as it was capable of seeing the light.

At last the long night wore away; as they passed Lyons, with its gleaming lights and its broad river; the first faint grey of dawn was quivering on the horizon, and gradually the pale morning twilight began to steal into the railway carriage, falling with a most ghastly effect on the faces of the sleepers—Noir, with his hard, grim features, Rouge serenely comfortable and animal-like, a priest with a heavy face, which nevertheless looked quite spiritual compared with the old captain's, and four average Frenchmen in every variety of night *déshabillé* and posture. Donovan glanced at them curiously, then, with that shivering misery which invariably accompanies the dawn, he once more looked out over the grey landscape. His cough began to be troublesome, nor did his discomfort end till the sun had risen; in the early morning, when they stopped for a minute at Orange, he dashed out of the carriage, held face and hands under the pump on the platform, and, somewhat refreshed by the cold water, got in again, to endure as well as he could the long day of travelling.

A night's rest at Nice set him up again, however, and he was as eager as either of his companions to go on to Monaco the next morning. The day, too, was so gloriously bright, and the air so exhilarating, that he fancied himself stronger than he really was. Nor was the exquisite scenery altogether wasted on him; it is to be doubted whether it has any effect on the *habitués* of Monte Carlo who daily pass through it, but Donovan was a stranger, not yet seized with the gaming mania, which seems to destroy all the nobler faculties.

Leaving Nice behind them, with its green hills and clustering white villas, they sped on through a very paradise of beauty. To the right lay the Mediterranean, with its wonderfully deep blue, broken here and there by the tiniest foam-wreathed breakers, gleaming whiter than snow; to the left rose the Maritime Alps with their softly mantling olive groves, while in the distance every now and then a snowy peak stood out clearly against the blue sky.

The three Englishmen certainly took their own fashion of enjoying it all, there was no studying of Murray or Bædeker, not a single exclamation of wonder or admiration. Rouge looked sleepily at the sea, and thought of his voyages in the *Metora*; Noir, who for the last day or two had been engrossed with his "system," and had done nothing but cover sheets of paper with dots, barely looked up from his employment; Donovan looked at all the beauty silently, with no lack of admiration, but with a certain sadness, his one definite thought being how much Dot would have enjoyed it. In a very short time they reached their destination; old Monaco on its rocky promontory, new Monaco, with its gay white houses and red-tiled roofs, Monte Carlo, with its gorgeous casino—

all lay as it were in a nutshell. Strange little Principality! one of the most ancient in Europe, originally a sort of garden of Eden, but now a perfect hot-bed of vice! Noir, who knew the place well, had his own reasons for avoiding the fashionable Condamine. He took his companions to an out-of-the-way hotel in old Monaco, where at the expense of a stiff climb they would be free from some of the objections of the more frequented quarter.

Before long they had set off for an afternoon at Monte Carlo, all three in good spirits; Noir with implicit faith in the system of play which he was about to try; Donovan exulting in the sense of novelty and excitement; Rouge ready to be amused by anything, and eager to try his luck so far as the restricted allowance which his son made him would permit. Driving up the long hill they were set down at last at the entrance to the casino. This, then, was the goal they had been making for, this the place where fortunes were won—or lost, this the refuge for all who craved excitement, for all who would fain banish thought. It felt half dream-like to Donovan, a palace of the genii, transported straight from one of the "Arabian Nights." Passing into the beautiful vestibule, with its great marble columns, gorgeously decorated roof and walls, and handsome mosaic floor, the impression grew upon him, but was speedily dashed into the world of cold realities by a word from Noir.

"Come, we won't waste time. You'll have to give your name at the *bureau*, and get your ticket. Of course, by-the-way, you're twenty-one? Else they won't admit you."

"All right," replied Donovan. "I was of age last spring," and therewith came memories which brought a look of hard resentment to his face.

Having given the name which he used, he picked up his pink admission-card, and followed his companions through the double swing-doors into the *Salle de Jeu*. After all, even in this enchanted palace, thoughts would intrude themselves. Would this journey to Monte Carlo prove less satisfactory than he had expected?

It is a strange sight that *Salle de Jeu*. Its richly decorated walls, its heavy square pillars, coloured and begilt in the Alhambra style, form the setting to a dark picture. How many wretched faces, pale with despair, are reflected each day in those mirrors! how many victims pace restlessly up and down the slippery par-quiet floor, never satisfied with gain, half crazed with loss; and yet with what persistency all throng round the tables, a curiously mixed multitude, when one pauses to study them—people of all ranks and ages: florid-looking Germans, sharp-faced Frenchmen, dark, vindictive Italians, handsome Russians, hard-featured Englishmen; women, too, in almost as large a proportion as men, and staking with quite as much *sang-froid*. Round every table sit the favoured few who have secured chairs, behind these stand the eager crowd absorbed in watching the whirling roulette-wheel, or the dealing of the cards, and on the outskirts of all linger the mere lookers-on; Americans "doing Europe," and including Monte Carlo in their list of things to be seen, pale-faced invalids from Mentone, English tourists of every description, who come to see this sight which happily is not to be met with in many places. A questionable proceeding though in some ways is this looking on, and yet to those who really study the gamblers the sight can hardly fail to teach a very grave lesson. Only, to anyone who expects pleasure in the mere sight, the disappointment would be great. Monte Carlo merely heard of is one thing, Monte Carlo seen is a revelation of sin, of infatuation, of all that is most sad and pitiable; a black spot in creation which does indeed make the on-looker thankful for all existing purity and goodness, but which, at the same time, cannot fail to sober and sadden.

The three companions quickly separated, Rouge remaining at one of the roulette-tables in the outer room, Noir steadily settling himself at the first trente-et-quarante table, and in course of time securing a chair, Donovan wandering restlessly from place to place. He had no faith in any system, though Noir had tried hard to convert him to his, but, although he was usually as successful by luck in games of chance as he was by cleverness in games of skill, his customary good fortune seemed now to have deserted him. Before long he had not only lost a great deal more than was at all convenient, but had conceived a strong dislike to the whole thing. Dispirited by his unbroken losses, he felt at once that there was nothing here to satisfy him, nothing to call out his faculties; for he was more than a mere gambler, he was a first-rate card-player, and to him half the pleasure of gaming lay in the sense of power, the exultation in his own skill. In spite of all the talk about "systems," he saw that the ruling goddess at Monte Carlo was blind chance; she had not dealt kindly with him, he would waste no more time or money in her gorgeous shrine.

But now that all excitement was over he began to feel unbearably weary, he threw himself down on the crimson velvet ottoman in the middle of the gaming-room, idly scanning the passers-by, men old and young; croupiers just released from their wearisome duties, and leaving the room with tired faces from which all other expression had died; the servants of the casino in their blue and red livery; the ever-shifting throng of gamblers; the extravagantly-dressed women. Realising at length that his peace was in danger of molestation, he rose to go, and found his way across the vestibule to the beautiful music-hall, where the finest orchestra in Europe is made a bait to draw great crowds to the casino. Wearily he leant back in one of the luxurious arm-chairs and listened to the closing strains of a grand symphony. The concert was nearly over; he was so weary that he almost fell asleep, but in, the last piece suddenly came to himself with a thrill of pain. With exquisite expression, with unrivalled delicacy of light and shade, the orchestra was playing a selection from "Don Giovanni," and now through the great hall there rang Dot's favourite air "Vedrai Carino."

It did him good in spite of the pain. When the audience dispersed, and he strolled out into the gardens, a child's pure gentle face haunted him; there among the palms, and aloes, and flowering cactus two visions of the past were with him, Dot's radiant beauty, and the quiet maidenly grace of a stranger whom he had involuntarily taken as his standard of what a woman should be. From what evil these two guardian angels shielded him who can say?

Before long he wisely went in search of the old captain, whom he found in low spirits, having lost every five-franc piece in his possession.

"We've both had enough of this," said Donovan, not sorry to have the old man's arm to lean on. "I'm about cleared out too, and, what's worse, I feel awfully seedy."

"Humph!" ejaculated the captain. "In for a second go of inflammation, I'll be bound."

"Well, Rouge, if I am," said Donovan, slowly, "you'll just have to bolt and bar the door and nurse me yourself. Do you understand?"

The captain nodded assent, and little more

was said as they made their way back to the hotel.

The surmise proved perfectly true, however, and that night Donovan was again tossing to and fro in weary misery, haunted by whirling roulette wheels and stony-faced croupiers, raving about the endless losses and the tantalizing gains which always eluded his grasp. The relapse was the natural consequence of all the fatigue he had gone through, and had it not been for the old captain's devoted though rough nursing, and for the care of an exceedingly clever French doctor, he would most likely have sunk under it.

However, he struggled through, and woke one morning, after a long sleep, to realise for the first time his position. There he was lying as weak as any baby, surrounded by mosquito net curtains, in an odd-looking foreign room; there was poor Waif lying at the foot of the bed, keeping anxious guard over him; there was Rouge sitting by the open window smoking. Where was he? What was this new place? Not Drury Lane, for the dingy green paper was changed to a gorgeous blue one, and the ceiling was decorated, or defaced, with bluewash studded with glaring white stars, in the middle of which grew by some strange anomaly a great clump of red and yellow roses. Donovan, though not artistic, was strangely irritated by looking at the horrid daub. He called the old captain to him.

"So I've been ill again," he said, interrogatively.

"Very," replied Rouge. "In fact, milord, we as good as gave you up at one time, you wouldn't believe what an anxious time I've had of it, with Noir all day long up at that casino, and no one here who could speak a word of English."

"You have been nursing me?"

"Well, of course, what else could I do?" said Rouge.

"Thank you, captain," said Donovan, adding resolutely, after a minute's pause, "I shall get well now."

He was as good as his word, and from that day recovered rapidly; not that he cared much to get well, but he was anxious to free himself from the state of dependence he was now in, for dependence was uncongenial to his nature, and to submit to rough and ready attendance is never pleasant. Before many days had passed he was up and dressed, just able to drag himself across the room, and to relieve the monotony of the long hours by such amusement as he could find at either of the windows. One of these faced the Place du Palais. There just opposite to him he could see the Prince's Palace, could count the slow minutes by the clock in the tower, speculate when the cannon and the great pile of cannon-balls would be used, study the two sentries who, in their red and blue uniforms, kept guard over the entrance gate, and watch the few passers-by. From the other window a much wider view was obtained. Here he could see the whole of the beautiful bay, and the exquisite loveliness of the place made him long to quit his room.

And so the days dragged on, and little by little he regained his strength, would crawl out to the almost deserted Promenade St. Barbe, and sit on one of the green benches under the plane-trees, or, passing through the curious old archway which leads by a footpath from old to new Monaco, he would stretch himself out on the low stone wall, and rest among a sort of jungle of flowering cactus and pink geranium, while before him stretched a glorious panorama; the beautiful blue of the Mediterranean, Monaco with its gay-looking houses, the mountains skirting the water here clothed with olive groves, there craggy, bare, and brown, or glistening pearly grey in the sunlight. Then just facing him, half way up the mountain side, the pretty little town of Roccabruna, till—the slope of the mountain hiding Mentone and its bay—the chain gradually lessened, and ended in the long low promontory of Bordighera. Only one conspicuous object stood out always as a blot on the fair landscape—the casino, with its gilded roof and its two minarets.

Donovan had wisely resolved to keep clear of modern Monaco, but he began rather to weary of the narrow bounds of the old town. True he had, as usual, made friends among the children; his favourite resting-place on the wall happened to be on the way to the school, and troops of little brown-eyed, bare-headed girls and boys passed him every day, and soon learnt to crowd round the strange English gentleman and his wonderful dog, and to bring him presents of flowers or unripe nespoli. But, as he grew stronger, he began to hate the feeling of imprisonment, until, happening one morning to notice a little boat on the sea with its white lateen sail, he conceived the happy idea of taking a daily cruise. The old captain was always ready to accompany him, and the hours which they spent in the *Ste. Dévote*, as their boat was named, did each of them untold good.

Meanwhile each evening Noir, returning about eleven o'clock, when the casino closed, would bring in one or two acquaintances who, not satisfied with the day's gambling, were anxious for play. In this manner Donovan made an easy living.

Noir tried in vain to induce him to go once more to Monte Carlo; he himself had been remarkably lucky, and he rarely let a day pass without remonstrating with Donovan on what he alternately called his "cowardice," his "laziness," and his "puritanical fanaticism."

This last accusation was so novel that it called forth one of Donovan's rare laughs.

"Come, this is quite a new line," he said, when Noir's tirade was ended. "You are the first person in the world who ever gave me such an honourable name. Zealous folks have addressed me as 'infidel dog,' and 'blind atheist,' and 'miserable agnostic,' but 'fanatic Puritan' is a title to which I never dreamt of aspiring! In the strength of it you must allow me to gang my ain gait!"

"Please yourself," said Noir, crossly. "Do

you know Berrogain's last name for you—for the young man who is too virtuous to be ensnared? You are the young Bayard, the——"

"He's welcome to call me what he pleases," interrupted Donovan, sharply. "All I know or care for is that he loses hundreds of francs to me every evening we play. It's not the least good talking. You'll never see me in that *Salle de Jeu* again. You with your system, and Berrogain with his luck, may do very well. Fortune wasn't so kind to me, and I'd rather depend on my own brains."

Sweepstakes ended the discussion by reiterated injunctions to "be gentle," and the words, coming in after a hot dispute, amused both speakers, and really did put a stop to the quarrel.

Noir finished his lunch, and set off for his afternoon at Monte Carlo, leaving his father and Donovan to such amusement as they could find in a long sail in the *Ste. Dévote*. Strangely enough, however, it so happened that the infallible "system" failed dismally on that very afternoon. Noir was singularly unfortunate, lost almost all that he had previously won, and returned to the hotel at night crestfallen and dispirited. He had burnt his fingers, and for the time had lost all desire to risk a fresh effort.

Rather sulkily he consented the next morning to go for a walk with Donovan, and, *déjeuner* over, the two set out towards the quaint little town of Roccabruna. As they passed through old Monaco and down the sunny road, a furious rattling attracted their notice. All the small boys of the place had armed themselves with impromptu policemen's rattles made of odd bits of wood and iron, and were swinging them round with frightful energy.

"What is all this infernal row about?" grumbled Noir.

Donovan, rather amused by the comical effect of the energetic *gamins* and their clumsy rattles, accosted a brown-eyed boy, and asked him the meaning of it all.

"It is the Holy Thursday, monsieur," was the answer. "We crush the bones of the wicked Judas, the betrayer. This evening, in the church, it will be very beautiful. The priests will wash our feet, the lights will be extinguished, and all the people will crush the bones of Judas. A great noise it will be, monsieur. It will resemble the thunder!"

Donovan. rejoined Noir with a bitter smile on

his face. This then was Christianity! They walked on in perfect silence.

The day was gloriously fine and bright, the April air soft and balmy, the atmosphere in that state of almost intoxicating clearness only to be met with in the South. Certainly the two men were a strange contrast to their surroundings; the elder grim, clouded, dissatisfied, the younger worn with suffering, weary with the weariness of a life-long unrest, and bearing on his handsome features that peculiar expression of constant inward struggle which often gives pathos to the hardest face.

Around them were the thick olive groves, above the clear deep blue of the cloudless sky. It was a paradise of peace and loveliness that these two were treading together. How far it influenced them it would be hard to say, but probably both owed more to it than they knew. Roccabruna, with its cavernous houses and quaint archways, did not greatly interest them. They had come for exercise rather than for lionising and, contented with a very brief survey of the little antique place, they struck off to the left, along a somewhat rough and rugged mule-path, and walked on silently in the direction of Mentone, each bend bringing them to fresh loveliness, to glimpses of new rocky heights, to little silvery impetuous waterfalls, to different views of the exquisite coast and of the Mediterranean, which at its very bluest spread out before them in calm beauty. At last Donovan spoke.

"Have you had enough of Monaco yet? Shall we go?"

"Certainly, I'll go to-morrow, if you'll come back on the old footing to London," said Noir, with a quick glance at his companion.

"'To that you've had your answer already," he replied, coldly. "I shall never go back to the old life. I told you so."

"Saint!" said Noir, with his most disagreeable sneer.

"Saint or devil, I'm not going to do it," said Donovan, his voice rising. "Call me what names you like, but understand once for all that when I say a thing I mean it."

Noir knew that this was true enough, knew, as he looked at the firm resolute face, that he might more easily move the rocks at Monaco than turn this fellow from his purpose.

"A month at Paris might not be amiss," he suggested, after a pause. "Berrogain is going back next week; he's made his fortune now—broke the bank yesterday."

"I am ready to go, then," said Donovan. "The sooner we're out of this place the better."

"Paris would not be bad," mused Noir, half to himself; "we shall come in for the meeting at Chantilly; perhaps induce Darky Legge to come over. Yes, that'll do; are you agreed?"

"Agreed? Oh, yes," replied Donovan, shortly; and then, as they passed a little wayside chapel in the midst of an olive grove, he said, with an abrupt change of tone, "Let us rest here; one doesn't often get shade like this."

And throwing himself down under one of the gnarled old trees, with arms crossed pillow-wise beneath his head, he lay watching the glimpses of blue through the graceful network of branches above him, and the still bluer depth of sea down below, against which the dark outlines of an iron cross stood out distinctly. Noir filled his pipe, and sat with his back against the trunk of the olive, not caring to attempt any further conversation.

"Life," thought the elder man, depressed by his losses, "was particularly worthless and uninteresting just at that time." "Life," thought the younger, perplexed by his increasing difficulties, troubled within and without, " life was more than a man could well stand; it was weary, and profitless, and utterly hateful."

Thus they mused, each following his natural bent, each calling that "life" which was in reality death, each wondering that they found it so barren and worthless. Neither could understand that the very sense of insaticty which came to them in their selfish lives was the token of those higher affinities within them, those faint needings and longings for the Omnipresent Fire Divine, which He can—nay, surely *does*, everywhere kindle.

By-and-by, the one with a shrug, the other with a sigh, the reveries were ended, the burden of the so-called " life " was taken up once more; the two walked on slowly, past the beautiful villas and the fragrant orange groves, to Mentone.

CHAPTER VI.

LOSING SELF TO FIND.

Man-like is it to fall into sin,
Fiend-like is it to dwell therein,
Christ-like is it for sin to grieve,
God-like is it all sin to leave.
From the German. LONGFELLOW.

ELEVEN o'clock on a May morning, the bright sunshine peeping in obliquely through the *persiennes*, and lighting up the conventional French bed-room, with its wardrobe, mirror, writing-table, and gilt clock, also a well-worn, brown portmanteau, and a white and tan fox-terrier stretched at full length on the hearth-rug. Down below in the street there was the rumbling of wheels, the busy, morning traffic, occasionally the cheerful voices of busy Parisians as they passed by, occupied, no doubt, but not pressed and hurried as Londoners are.

These were the sights and sounds which first

greeted Donovan on a day which he was never to forget, a day every detail of which was burnt in upon his brain with the ineffaceable brand of suffering. He woke late, rang the bell for his coffee, and then lay musing. He was a rich man; the sensation was strange. A year ago he had been cast adrift, friendless, almost penniless; he had started with hardly any possession in the world, except the brown portmanteau and the fox-terrier which met his gaze from the other side of the room; now he was rich, a well-to-do man, for not many hours ago, when the faint dawn was just beginning to break, he had won a fortune at baccarat. In spite of Ellis's wickedness, in spite of life-long injustice, he had done well for himself.

And yet, after all, did it make so very much difference? Was this great success, this unparalleled good fortune, so really worth having? His heart did not feel any lighter, life did not look more inviting when he got up that day. At the actual time of his triumph his bliss had been complete, his one passion rode rampant over everything. A splendid game, a fortune at stake, a fortune which he by his marvellous play had won! Everything else was forgotten, care for the time cast aside, weariness lost, insatiety filled, the hollow unsatisfactory world became a temporary paradise!

But now it had passed, and the dull weight of existence pressed on him once more. Was he so much better off than poor M. Berrogain even, the man by whose losses he had been enriched? Was the loser many degrees more depressed than the winner?

He was just about to leave his room, when, with a hasty knock, Noir Frewin entered.

"Milord," he said, quickly, "you're wanted in the next room; there's no end of a scene going on—Berrogain's wife in floods of tears; her husband has made off no one knows where, and, from a few written words he left, seems to intend suicide."

Donovan gave a dismayed start, made a gesture of horror.

"What!" he gasped, in a voice which contrasted oddly with Noir's off-hand manner.

"Simply what I say," said Noir. "Don't look as if you'd already seen his ghost; of course it's a bad business, but come in and see the wife, and don't put her down as a widow till we've found all the facts."

With an impatient movement, Donovan pushed past the speaker, and in a dazed bewildered way found himself in the room where the old captain was trying to say something cheering to a little dark-eyed woman, whose piquant face was wet with tears and pale with anxiety.

"Here is M. Donovan," said Rouge, paternally; "he has a good heart, madame—he will help you."

"Ah! monsieur," she cried, turning to him with streaming eyes, "listen, at least listen, to my trouble. In the night my husband returns, he tells me he is ruined—he, the fortunate, has been ruined—all the fortune he made at Monaco lost—gone. I ask him how, and he tells me it is the young Englishman, the M. Donovan, of whom so much was said at the club—he it is who has caused the ruin. Oh! monsieur," and here the poor little woman's voice was broken with sobs, "you, who are so good, so prudent, you whom they called the young Bayard, *sans peur et sans reproche*—oh! monsieur, is it possible that you did it? They said you were too good for Monaco, but oh! monsieur, it is worse to ruin others than to ruin yourself. Think, monsieur—think what it means; you have driven my husband away in despair—he may even now be no more. Oh! *mon Dieu! mon Dieu!* Think if the Seine be flowing over him!

Monsieur, speak to me, help me; it is you who have brought us this evil—speak, monsieur!"

Throughout the impassioned address Donovan had stood rigidly still; he felt sick with horror, the strength went out of his arms, for the time he really was paralysed by the appalling consciousness of the responsibility resting on him. He had, perhaps—nay, probably—driven a man to suicide, ruined and widowed the poor woman before him. Was he much better than a murderer?

"Speak, monsieur!" reiterated Madame Berrogain through her tears.

He turned at last to Rouge appealingly.

"I can't speak to her; you must——"

"M. Donovan is much moved," said the old captain; "he tells me to speak for him; be assured, madame, that he will do all in his power; he is good and——"

"*Do!*" interrupted Donovan, with a sudden return of strength and vehemence—"is there anything to do? Only tell me of any hope that all this is not true, that your fears are groundless——"

"Alas! monsieur, but who can say?" sobbed Madame Berrogain. "He is gone—gone—see his last words!" and she held out to him a sheet of paper, on which was written in French:

"*My wife,—I cannot bear this intolerable misery. I must fly from all most dear, and seek a refuge in darkness; life is ended for me. Farewell! Thy unhappy one,*—BERROGAIN."

To Donovan the words conveyed little hope; still he clung to the idea that there might possibly be time to hinder this rash act, and with the hope all the man within him re-asserted itself.

"Madame," he said, earnestly, "all that can be done I will do. We will advertise in all the papers; I will seek your husband in every place in Paris where we know of any chance of finding him. I will find him if I die in doing it."

In spite of his bad French and limited means of expression, in spite too of his grave stern face, Madame Berrogain understood the depth of the promise, and knew that the man who had ruined her husband was yet a man to be trusted.

"And you think there is hope," she cried. "Oh! monsieur, you think there is really hope?"

He struggled hard to speak, and, with his habitual control, forced himself at last to say,

"Be comforted, madame, I will do everything

that is possible; hope for the best, and to-night we will bring you word. You shall know all that has been done."

"Monsieur is good," said the poor wife, wiping her eyes. "He will work, and I—I will pray to our Lady."

In a few minutes more she rose to leave, and, with her *bonne* beside her, went back to her desolate rooms.

Donovan, as soon as she had left, drew paper and ink to him, and sitting down began to write rapidly. Rouge watched the forcible characters as they were traced with a sort of vague wonder and bewilderment. A few moments before his companion had seemed utterly unnerved, now his iron face and the swift precision of his movements made him seem like a machine."

"What are you doing?" asked the captain, curiously.

"Advertisements," was the laconic reply, spoken in the voice which more than anything tells of a mind strained to the highest tension, half sharp, half weary.

Five minutes of writing, and then Donovan rose, snatched up his hat and opened the door. The captain stopped him.

"Let me come with you, lad," he said, in his good-humoured voice.

"Yes, come," said Donovan, with a shade of relief in his tone; and then the two hurried down the stairs and out into the sunny street. Just outside the door they found Noir sauntering up and down with his pipe; he stopped them to ask their errand, gave his advice as to putting the matter into the hands of the police, and then turned away with his usual cool nonchalance, under which was, nevertheless, hidden more sympathy than might have been expected.

"Milord is the very worst person for such a thing to come to," he mused; "a man without a conscience wouldn't have troubled himself to think twice of the matter. Now Donovan's as likely as not to go raving mad if this Berrogain isn't found."

At present there were no signs of the anticipated "madness;" Donovan was perfectly quiet and clear-headed, he walked on swiftly with Rouge beside him, setting about his disagreeable work in the most business-like way. In spite of his English pronunciation too, there was that about him which obliged the various officials to receive his orders with civility and obedience.

Not to think—that was his one great effort, but the horror of the overhanging dread would obtrude itself,—or if by his strong will he banished it for a time, it was only to be conscious, through the hard matter-of-fact absence of feeling which he forced himself into, of the dull nameless weight at his heart.

It was about four in the afternoon when they reached the Pont d'Arcole, and the old captain was beginning to feel both hungry and tired. He looked at his companion then questioningly, and saw a little additional sternness about his face. Groups of men were leaning over the parapet watching the river; Donovan too paused for a moment and looked down at the sparkling water; Rouge fancied he saw him shudder, but he did not speak, and walked on again more rapidly than before.

"Where next?" asked the captain, anxiously.

"To the Morgue," said Donovan, in a firm but very low voice.

They went on in silence, and before long found themselves in the little crowd which was continually passing up and down the steps and through the doors of the small insignificant building which is dedicated to so painful a purpose.

"I will wait here for you," said Rouge, for he rather shrank from going inside, and Donovan, without a word, left him and pushed his way in with the eager crowd.

The waiting seemed long to the old captain; he began to wonder whether his companion had found poor Monsieur Berrogain in that dread room within, and anxiously scanned the faces of those who came out. Soldiers in shabby uniforms, women in their snowy white caps, men of all ranks and ages, sometimes even little children in arms.

At length, in this motley but cheerful and unconcerned crowd, came the face which Rouge was waiting for, a curious contrast to every other, stern, and sad, and white to the very lips.

The captain was startled.

"Good heavens! milord," he cried, "you have not found him, have you?"

Donovan shook his head, and clutched at his companion's arm to steady himself.

"Why, you're ill," said the captain. "Within an ace of fainting."

"Nonsense, nothing of the kind," panted Donovan. "Only let us get away from this place," and with Rouge's assistance he crossed the road, but there, finding his strength failing, was obliged to lean up against the railings, even to cling to them for support. The horrible sight, the dread of what he might possibly find, had completely unnerved him, for one dreadful moment, too, he had fancied that he recognized M. Berrogain, and, in spite of the subsequent relief at his mistake, he could not recover from the shock.

"Only don't let's have a scene," was his answer to all Rouge's suggestions, and at last, with the old captain's help, he managed to get as far as the entrance to the garden east of Notre Dame, and to rest on a bench under the trees.

Everything there was bright and peaceful, the grey old church, with its pinnacles and flying buttresses, the fresh green of the spring leaves, the sunshine streaming down with that gaiety and brightness which seem specially to characterise Paris, and here and there a little child at play with its *bonne* in attendance. Once a tiny, fairy-like little thing, whose white dress showed that she was "dedicated to the Virgin," stole up to Donovan—she had watched him with a sort of fascination ever since he had thrown himself down on the bench. Was it merely compassion for one who seemed ill, or was it that peculiar attraction which Donovan possessed for children? The tiny maid, prompted by some unknown influence, at any rate resolved to do her best for him, and, with her little quick fingers, began gathering *marguerites*, then, grasping the bunch with her two fat little hands, she toddled up to the silent figure, and, with a premonitory pat to arouse him, laid her offering on his knees.

"See then, monsieur, the pretty flowers, they are all for you."

He put his hand for a moment on the dimpled one of his tiny friend, and, as well as he could, thanked her, but the daring little mite was soon pursued by an indignant nurse.

"Mademoiselle Gabrielle, come away this moment. Ah! little wicked one! I dare not take my eyes off thee for a single instant!"

So Mademoiselle Gabrielle was led away in disgrace, but looked round nevertheless to kiss her hand, and to nod her pretty little head in farewell, and Donovan followed her with his eyes, with a great pain at his heart. The little child's gift touched him strangely, it had come in such a moment of tumult and horror, when self was feeling so utterly hateful, the weight of dread responsibility so heavy, and this fairy-like creature had pitied him, liked him, he was grateful with the almost passionate gratitude of humility.

For it was a very terrible thing this that had come to him, this woe that he had unthinkingly brought about. He was very young still, only just two and twenty, and in spite of his wretched roving life, in spite of the bitter misanthropy he professed, there was still in him the chivalry of all strong natures, the nobleness which must protect what is weak; little children and women he looked upon with a sort of devotion; from his very childhood it had been so, the ideal of motherhood, the passionate love for Dot, had been the ruling motives of his life. The ideal of the wife was still unformed, he had never loved, or even fancied that he loved any woman. Only when the thought of home-life came to him, as now and then it would, when he saw the outer side of the lives of others, the vision of the grey-eyed stranger whom he had met in Hyde Park would rise up before him, the tender, bright, womanly woman, whose purity and sweetness had had such a powerful influence over him—had even helped to keep him straight when he had been exposed to the countless snares of Monaco.

Because of this strong reverence for women, the scene of the morning had been specially painful to him. The poor wife's misery, which must have haunted anyone with a heart, haunted him with a pain and shame almost intolerable. But fortunately he was—notwithstanding all his failings—brave and manly, he struggled now with his weakness, and began to make his plans for further searching—that "doing" which was such a relief to his burdened mind.

"We will come to one of Duval's places and have some dinner," was his first voluntary remark to the old captain, about as sensible and matter-of-fact a proposal as could have been made.

So they went to the nearest of the restaurants, and Rouge's devoted attendance was rewarded by the privilege of ordering whatever he liked, while Donovan gulped down enough food to support him in his work, conquering his utter disinclination till he had satisfied his conscience, and then calling Waif to devour the plentiful leavings.

After that came another deliberate plunge into the crowded streets, another long continued but utterly vain search for the lost man. Ceaseless inquiries, endless hurryings to and fro, once or twice a supposed clue to M. Berrogain's whereabouts, to be followed by temporary hope and bitter disappointment.

Once, as the evening wore on, Donovan stopped at a *café* on one of the boulevards and made the old captain have a cup of *café noir*, even permitted the *petit verre* without a remonstrance; but this time he was too sick at heart to force himself to take anything, hope had almost died out since his last disappointment, and the numbing paralysing horror was beginning to overwhelm him again.

Rouge, as he sipped his coffee contentedly, happened to look across the little marble table at his silent companion, and then for the first time realised that the day's anxiety had been something far severer than he could comprehend. For Donovan's face was worn and haggard, grey with that strange ghastliness which only comes on such young faces in times of great exhaustion; the firm mouth betrayed suffering, the eyes, though feverishly alive to all that was passing, had a painfully despairing look in them.

"Donovan, lad," said Rouge, anxiously, "you will come home now, won't you?"

"You go home, captain," he answered,

"you've had a long day, I? no, I can't come yet. I must see whether the police have found anything, and I must see *her*—Madame Berrogain."

"Milord, you'll only be ill again," remonstrated the old man, "you'll do for yourself one of these days."

"That means I shall do the best thing that could be done," said Donovan, with an odd sudden smile, followed by a quick sigh. "But you see, captain, this coil of flesh is terribly tough. Good night, go home and rest."

He pushed back his chair suddenly, threw down a franc beside the captain's cup, and before his companion could remonstrate had walked away rapidly alone.

At length, wearily and quite hopelessly, he went to see if any of the agencies he had set to work had been successful in tracing M. Berrogain. He had some minutes to wait in the *bureau* of the chief official, but at last a small sharp-faced man appeared with a paper in his hand, and an all-pervading odour of garlic, which was quite beneath the dignity of his position.

"You are come to inquire for Théodore Berrogain, disappeared mysteriously since the

LOSING SELF TO FIND. 165

hour of 4 a.m. Good! I think we have traced him."

Donovan did not speak, only breathed more quickly and clenched and unclenched his hands, his usual sign of strong feeling.

"Inquiries have been made, and this is the result,—at the *Gare d'Orléans* the *chef* states that a man answering to your description, much above the usual height, pale, with thick light hair and moustaches, and a cast in one eye, was seen early this morning at the station; the official at the ticket office also remembers him, and will undertake to swear that he issued a ticket to him for Bordeaux, third class. Acting upon this, monsieur, we have telegraphed to the officials at Bordeaux; the train by which it is supposed M. Berrogain left Paris reaches Bordeaux this evening at 10.30, it will be met by our agents there, and they will telegraph to us the movements of your friend."

Doubtless the man thought the "friendship" was a remarkable one—one must love a companion much to be so particularly anxious about him, and Donovan's intense relief, though so thoroughly undemonstrative, was nevertheless apparent even to the sleepy official. He arranged to call early the next morning for further tidings, and then hurried away to relieve poor Madame Berrogain's anxiety.

Anyone who knows the sensation of a sudden respite, the removal of an intolerable load, the relief from oppressing fear, will understand with what feelings Donovan hastened along the gas-lit streets. He was treading on air; new life was coursing through his veins; the very consciousness of free unburdened existence was in itself exquisite. And then came the satisfaction of imparting his hopeful news to the poor wife, amid a torrent of fervent thanks, tears, incoherent blessings, and exclamations of relief.

He tried to cut the scene short, and it was not till he was standing at the open door that he placed in Madame Berrogain's hands a small piece of paper.

"I give this to you, madame, because I think it is better so. To-morrow I shall go to your husband, and I will tell him what you hold for him."

He would have moved to the staircase, but Madame Berrogain laid her hand on his arm. She had glanced rapidly at the paper, and now the tears were streaming down her cheeks.

"No, no, monsieur, this is too good! This

must not be! Take it back, monsieur, I implore."

"Madame asks what is impossible," he replied, with his rare and beautiful smile. "One day's possession is sufficient for me; only, if I might be allowed one suggestion, I would say that it were better used for madame's own needs, not risked again at baccarat."

"Ah! God bless you! God guard you!" exclaimed the little wife, clasping her hands together. "Monsieur, I shall remember you always. On my knees I shall remember you, believe it. Ah! heaven, if all were but like you!"

He submitted to having his hand pressed in both hers for a moment, then, bowing low, he hastened away.

After that, naturally enough came the reaction. He was dreadfully worn out, and apart from his relief, everything that faced him in the future was most painful. For this great shock had shown him what a hateful life he was leading, and he knew that it must be forsaken.

He found the old captain in his room smoking, told him of Monsieur Berrogain's probable whereabouts, and then, with a sigh of great weariness, stretched himself at full length on the hearthrug. Before very long Noir came in, and having heard the news in his cool, uninterested way, remarked, carelessly,

"Well, I'm glad for your sake that the fellow's in the land of the living still. I suppose he's off to America?"

"He will be watched and arrested, if he attempts it," said Donovan. "To-morrow morning I shall start for Bordeaux. It is the only sure way of making all right to see him myself."

"Folly!" said Noir, crossly. "Why, the best thing he can do is to leave the country."

"Madame Berrogain might not agree with you."

"But the fellow's ruined. You know he can't live here."

"You are mistaken," said Donovan, quietly. "He is not ruined."

"What!" cried Noir, in a startled voice. "You mean that you have let him off, that you've been such an utter fool as to let those thousands slip through your fingers again?"

"Exactly—yes—such an utter fool," said Donovan, with a touch of satire.

"Well, milord, you're a softer fellow then than I thought. A woman's tears and an absurd scare lest a weak-minded wretch should have drowned himself, and you melt directly, become the generous hero of the piece, fling *largesse* to right and left, and walk off amid cheers and applause. I'd no idea you were so weak-minded! Besides, you know well enough you'll repent your bargain in a few days. As your favourite Monsieur Renan says, 'Most beautiful actions are done in a state of fever.' You'll recover and repent it."

"Do I seem feverishly excited?" asked Donovan, quietly. "And do I generally fail in deliberation?"

"Don't bother him now," interposed the old captain. "We've had an awful day of it."

"What in the world you did it for I can't conceive," said Noir, unheeding. "You who profess to rail at the injustice of life! you who call yourself a misanthrope! What induced you to spend your time on such a search? What does it matter to you if all the world is ruined?"

"I suppose, after all, I didn't hate the whole world," said Donovan, slowly, "or else the hatred was all needed in another direction."

Noir caught his meaning, and, because he could just recognise its humility and sad honesty, it roused all the evil in him; he knew that his companion was slipping away from him.

"And how does your moral highness propose to live if you refund the money you won?" The question was put with a contemptuous sneer.

"How I shall live, Noir," answered Donovan, gravely, "I cannot tell, but by gambling I shall not live."

"We shall see," said Noir, "when you recover from this state of fever. Why, do you think that in a moment like this you can end the strongest incentive of your life? You know perfectly well that you don't care a rush for anything except the cards."

"You've about hit it," said Donovan, "but," with a firmness which seemed to give treble force to each separate word, "*I will not play again.*"

For a minute both the Frewins were silent; both involuntarily looked at their companion as he lay, his thin skilful hands clasped over his dark hair, his face resolute and full of noble purpose; he was quietly renouncing all he had as yet cared for in life, all by which he could win admiration, success, pleasure, and these two men knew it. Rouge was the first to speak.

"Well, lad, we will do the best we can for you; you will stay on with us."

And then the look of struggle came back to Donovan's face; he rose hurriedly, and began to pace up and down the room, scarcely hearing what his companions said to him.

At last he stopped abruptly in his walk, and said, hoarsely,

"No, I can't stay, captain."

"Can't!—nonsense!" said Noir. "We don't part after a whole year together in this way."

"I must go," he repeated. "I dare not stay."

"Dare not!—what, we are so bad that we shall corrupt your moral highness! Oh! go then, by all means, and may you find friends more faithful and better suited to your lofty standard!"

"Frewin," said Donovan, very sadly, "you know well enough that it is myself I dare not trust. If you think that I could stay with you and all our own set, and yet keep to my word, well and good. But I could not do it; it will be hard any way, impossible like that."

"A few months ago you would have scorned to say anything was impossible."

"Well, I've been taken down a few pegs

since then, and now I do say it and mean it. Good night, Noir."

"When do you leave?"

"To-morrow by the 9.20. Good night and good-bye."

Noir took his hand for a moment, looked him full in the face, as though to read what was written there, then, with an impatient gesture, he turned away.

"Good-bye. I see we have done with each other."

Sweepstakes, waking up, screamed out his habitual greetings.

"Such a talkin', such a talkin', what a parcel of fools! Ain't you a fool!—ain't you a fool, milord!"

The old captain, with maudlin tears coursing down his cheeks, hurried after the retreating figure, and it was long before Donovan could quiet the piteous entreaties that he would change his mind, would stay at least a few days longer, or would promise to come back when he had seen M. Berrogain. Parting with his companions was a greater wrench than he had feared even; they had been very good to him, had nursed him through his illness with rough but very real care, and they were the only friends he had in the whole world. And yet he knew that he must leave them; they were inseparably bound up with the evil he was trying to free himself from—both must be renounced.

He took leave of Rouge that night, and early next day started on his solitary journey—solitary with the exception of Waif. The address he needed had been telegraphed to the official when he went to inquire on his way to the station, and it was a substantial relief to his anxiety to be able to repeat to himself the assurance of M. Berrogain's safety—"Hôtel Montré, Rue Montesquieu, Bordeaux." There was, however, just a little flatness and depression now that all was ended; he took his ticket, and then went into the *salle d'attente*, the "durance vile" which generally gives an Englishman a chafed caged feeling. As he paced up and down, too, there was a touch of far-off dread in his face—the dread of the unknown future, which of all expressions is one of the most painful to see.

Noir Frewin, suddenly entering the room in search of his late companion, caught the look and understood it; unprincipled as he was he could not help respecting a resolution which could so steadily persevere in direct opposition to personal wishes, and there was none of the malice of the previous night in his tone when he spoke.

Donovan turned hastily at the sound of his own name; he was ill-prepared just then for a repetition of the scornful upbraidings which he had borne silently a few hours ago. Noir saw that his arrival was not very welcome.

"I'm only come to see you off," he explained. "You're quite right, milord, after all; go and save yourself while you can."

"Saving is not the question," said Donovan, "even if I believed in such a thing; but at any rate one needn't do others harm."

"A change in your views, lad, since we first went into partnership," said Noir. "Your anger with whoever it was who had ruined you has cooled with time."

"His offence looks small now that I am the bigger brute," replied Donovan. Then, as the doors were thrown open, he put his arm within Noir's once more, and they went out together to the train.

"Good-bye, old fellow," he said, rather hoarsely, just before the final start; "let us hope my lungs won't give out again, or I shall be crying out for you."

"Till then we are best away from each other," said Noir, giving his hand a farewell grip. "Good-bye, Farrant. We part as we met, you see, in a railway-carriage."

The train moved off; Frewin, with a fierce sigh, turned away, and Donovan was whirled through the vast plains of central France, marvelling not a little how his companion had learnt his real name, the name which he had taken such pains to conceal.

Thirteen hours later and he was standing in the crowded *salle* at the Bordeaux Station; he was very tired, a trifle desolate too, alone among foreigners, alone with such a "howling wilderness" of a future as he fancied before him, the future of restraint which he had chosen. Waiting rather impatiently till the doors of the luggage-room should be opened, he scanned the faces of the crowd, the usual busy cheerful crowd of a French railway-station; a group of men whiling away the waiting-time with laughter and occasional snatches of song, two lovers sitting on a bench in the corner, whispering contentedly together, regardless of their surroundings, a fat rough-featured priest, with his shovel hat and starched bands, a respectable *bourgeois* and his wife, followed by a toddling bare-headed child.

Instinctively Donovan watched the little one. The mother turned round, saying playfully, "*Adieu! adieu!*" pretending to leave it; the child let them walk on a few steps, and then, with sudden dread of being left, ran at full speed after them with an eager "*Non, non, non,*" and grasped its mother's skirts; then both father and mother laughed, each took one of the tiny hands, and the three walked away together.

Home dramas all around him, love in all its forms and degrees—the friend's, the lover's, the mother's, the wife's! He sighed, and stooped down to pat Waif. Then followed the general rush into the adjoining room, he went to claim his portmanteau, and in a few minutes was out in the starlight, on his way to M. Berrogain.

His desolateness made him think of Dot, of the times when he too had had some one to love and protect. They were sad, but on the whole peaceful thoughts which came to him as he crossed the bridge, pausing for a moment to look at the long chain of lights marking out the crescent-shaped quays. She, the holy child of his memory, was at peace; it was perhaps well that she had passed away from him, he had not been fit to be near such purity and loveliness, and as she had grown older it was possible that he might have pained her—pained her by his unworthiness. That thought was intolerable. And so, unconsciously, he repeated to himself Noir Frewin's words—"We were better parted." Neither of them knew that the unselfishness and humility prompting the thought was drawing them to the Source of all love.

The walk was a long one, through broad well-built streets, past the theatre, on again into narrower and darker thoroughfares, till Donovan began to wonder whether the porter whom he had hired to carry his portmanteau, were not perhaps taking him by some roundabout way in the hope of extorting a larger *pourboire*. At last, turning to the left, they passed through a circular market-place, and down a narrow street with high dingy-looking houses.

"There, monsieur," said the porter, with a wave of the hand, "that is the Hôtel Montré."

Donovan saw at the corner the inevitable *Café Billard*, and upon the upper storeys the name of the hotel inscribed. The porter went on to the entrance, and Donovan, following, found himself in a paved courtyard with two mouldy-looking orange-trees growing in tubs, and a dim light proceeding from the room of the *concierge*. He inquired at once for M. Berrogain, and was relieved to find that he was known still by his real name. He was within too, had taken his key not five minutes before, would monsieur see him at once or be shown to his own room?

Donovan desired to see M. Berrogain at once, and, having dismissed his guide, was ushered by a pretty, little, white-capped servant up a dirty stone staircase, along a labyrinth of passages, then up again and through a corresponding labyrinth darker and dirtier than that below.

"Perhaps monsieur sleeps," suggested the little servant, glancing round as she paused at a door to the right. "It is very late," and she pretended to yawn.

"Knock and see," said Donovan, impatient of the delay.

A quick *entrez!* relieved his fears, and, taking

the candle from his conductress, he opened the door and found himself in a fairly comfortable room, where, extended on a shabby green velvet sofa, lay M. Berrogain, the *Figaro* in his hand, the *Gironde* lying at his feet. For a moment the thought would come, "He is unconcerned and comfortable enough; you need not have troubled about him." But while Donovan paused, the unconscious Frenchman glanced round; he had been absorbed in his paper, and had half forgotten that some one had knocked and been admitted; now catching sight so unexpectedly of the man who had ruined him, he sprang to his feet with a cry half of fear, half of passion.

"Ah! evil one, why do you pursue me?" he said, in trembling tones. "Would you remember a petty debt of two hundred francs when you have won a fortune from me? Stonyhearted wretch! would you pelt a fallen man? You have tracked me—you the rich the successful will hunt down the unfortunate for a miserable trifle such as that!"

"I am not rich," said Donovan, "nor are you unfortunate."

"Miserable Englishman!" cried out M. Berrogain. "Why do you mock me? You are come to drive me to despair, to death! Why could you not let me leave the country in peace? Why do you come with your grasping avarice to——"

"Listen, Berrogain," interrupted Donovan, in his firm sad voice. "I could not let you leave the country, because there is no need for you to go; I am not mocking you; be quiet and listen. To-morrow morning you can go back to your wife at Paris; she holds the fortune which you lost at baccarat."

They were standing by the draped mantelpiece; Donovan turned away as he spoke, and putting aside the muslin curtains looked down into the dimly-lighted street. He was not sorry to feel the fresh air upon his face.

There was a moment's silence, then M. Berrogain came forward and took his hand.

"My friend," he said, falteringly, "forgive what I have said; I was in despair. But this generosity—no—no, it cannot be, it cannot be."

"It *must* be," said Donovan, quietly.

"No, no; leave me enough to go on upon, or allow me six months' respite, I should be more than content with that."

"But I should not," said Donovan, decidedly.

"No, Berrogain, everything is settled, so do not let us waste words on the subject."

"But it is unheard of!" said M. Berrogain. "It is noble, generous, kind; but, my good friend, before you commit yourself, think how will you get on in the world if you act in such a way?"

"That," said Donovan, with a half smile, "is a question yet to be solved, but I do not mean to live by other men's losses. Enough has been said though about it all. Can one get anything to eat in this place? I'm furiously hungry!"

"Ah! but you are an Englishman!" said M. Berrogain, amused by the request. "There is a restaurant just opposite, let me come with you."

"To watch the voracious islander!" said Donovan, laughing. "To-night I shall keep up the national character. I could eat half a roast beef if there was a chance of getting it!"

"Ah! is it possible?" said the Frenchman. "And at this time of night, too!"

He did not think that the anxiety which he had caused could possibly have affected his companion's appetite on the previous day, and sat amusedly at the table, watching the absolute demolition of the largest piece of *Ros-bif rôti* which the restaurant could produce.

Then somewhere in the small hours Donovan found his way to the rather dingy wainscoted room which had been allotted him, and, in spite of the noisy orgies being carried on in the room below, was soon sleeping profoundly.

M. Berrogain left for Paris the next day, and Donovan went to the station with him, submitted to his demonstrative gratitude, and then turned away rather disconsolately to make the best of his new life. He wandered about the place for some little time, found his way into the beautiful Church of St. Michel, looked wonderingly and half pityingly at the groups of worshippers drawing their *prie-Dieu* up to the side altars, then sauntered out again, along the quays, among the tramways and trucks, the coils of rope and the chains, idly scrutinizing the closely-moored vessels and the busy work of lading or unlading, or coaling, which was going on. Everywhere work and business. And he too must work, he had been leading a wretched self-indulgent life, he would work now, indeed he must work to live. The question was what should he do, and where should he go?

He had rather a hankering after America, but that idea had to be given up, for he had not enough to pay his passage; it seemed to be a choice of trying for some situation in Bordeaux itself, or of going back to England, the chances of finding immediate employment being about equally small in either case. He decided at last to let fate choose his destination, and tossed up a *petit sou*—heads he was to go to England, and thus it fell.

With a half sigh he pocketed the coin, looked at his watch, and then hurried away to find out when the next steamer left for Liverpool. There was one that evening to his relief, and he hastened back to the Hôtel Montré, glad that his hours in its dingy rooms were numbered. The passage was being swept by the little white-capped maid-servant as he passed down it, and as he put his things together the refrain of the song she was singing floated in to him:

> "Oui, malgré ta philosophie
> L'amour seul peut charmer la vie."

Over and over it went, a tuneless little chant, and with strange persistency it rang in his ears long after, "L'amour seul!—l'amour seul!" Was it indeed that which could alone make life supportable? He was not quite the misanthrope he had considered himself, but had he any love for his kind? Many times he asked himself that question, as he stood on the deck of the steamer while it ploughed its way through the Bay of Biscay, or lay with Waif at his feet, like a recumbent crusader, looking up at the starry skies. Did he only not hate? —was there anything more active than that in his feeling towards the rest of the world?

All this time he had hardly realised the hardness of the task he had set himself. He had willed never to play again, and was quite at rest now that the resolution was made, for never in his whole life had he failed to do a thing which he had deliberately undertaken. His confidence in his own strength was boundless, and though he had reasonably enough seen the impossibility of still living with the Frewins, now that he had once broken with the old set he did not give a thought to other possible temptations.

And thus, perfectly satisfied with the strength of his will, and full of his new and good purposes, he was set down at Liverpool. Then followed a time of bitter disappointment; though he had just renounced a fortune, the world gave him the cold shoulder again, and his money began to evaporate, to disappear with the horrid rapidity which becomes so noticeable when we are counting by units instead of tens. And very soon came the temptation. He had been out all day in the weary useless search after work, the evening set in wet and chilly, as he passed down the gaslit streets to his cheerless lodging a familiar sound made him pause, he was passing a billiard-room—the sharp click of the balls, the eager voices, how natural it all sounded! He had taken no resolution against playing billiards. Why should he not relieve this intolerable dulness by an hour or two of amusement? A momentary struggle followed, then he pushed open the door and went in. How long he was there he could never clearly remember, but it was not until a substantial token of his wonted success lay before him that he realised the failure of his will. He, the strong and self-reliant, had yielded to the very first temptation, had failed most miserably. He dropped the cue, pushed away the money, and amid a chorus of surprise and inquiry strode out of the room.

Too completely dismayed and bewildered to find any relief in his usual custom of rapid walking, he went back to his wretched lodging, and there sat motionless in the summer twilight in blank silent despair. Everything was lost—friends, money, pleasure, worst of all, his confidence in himself. What was there left? Nothing, he said, but a wretched life that was far better ended, a despicable "I," that must struggle to find itself bread, because—only because of a dim, inexplicable, unreasonable idea that self-destruction was wrong. What possible good was there in his life to himself or to anyone else? He did not think then of his influence with the Frewins, he could only feel that he had cheated himself, failed in his purpose, sunk irrevocably in his own opinion; what guarantee was there, too, that his will would not fail again?

Two paws on his knee and a soft warm tongue licking his hand roused him at length.

"Oh! Waif," he exclaimed, with a great sigh, "if only I'd a tenth of your goodness, old dog!"

By-and-by he lit the gas, dragged out the tin of dog biscuits, and gave Waif his supper, glancing in between the mouthfuls at the advertisement columns of an open newspaper which lay on the table. Once the dog was kept begging for quite a minute, for his master had become absorbed in what he was reading.

"Wanted, as secretary to the —— Institute, a young man of good abilities, knowledge of book-keeping and a clear handwriting indispensable; salary £100. Apply in person, on the 15th or 16th, the President, —— Institute, Exeter."

Secretary!—surely he was well fitted for the post. Possibly, too, there would be less competition down in the quiet west-country; here in Liverpool his chance of success seemed infinitesimally small.

"Well, my dog," he said, almost cheerfully, as he threw down the next mouthful, "shall we set off together and try our luck? £100 a year would keep you in biscuits, so there's some reason in it, after all."

The necessary inquiry, however, into his resources showed him only too plainly that he had not enough money for the journey; after his present expenses had been paid, his worldly possessions would have dwindled down to a sum below the price of a third-class ticket to Exeter. His watch and chain had been in pawn ever since the day after his arrival; he had no other valuables, nothing by which he could raise money, nothing except—— His eye fell on Dot's little travelling-clock, and he started painfully. The idea of selling that had never occurred to him before. In all his wanderings it had been with him—it was almost the only thing he still had which had belonged to her; to part with it seemed unbearable, and especially so in this particular way. To take it deliberately with his own hands and bargain about it, to leave it—the very thing which she had touched, and fondled, and admired—in a pawnbroker's shop, to let the silvery cathedral chime which she had loved fall on the ears of strangers, it seemed like desecration! And only an hour ago the money he had so much needed had been his. If he had but taken it, all this difficulty would have been avoided. But then his better self made its voice heard.

"No, my little Dot, no," he said aloud; "better a thousand times that this should go than that I should have been doubly false to myself."

He did then what he very seldom ventured to do—drew his little miniature of Dot from its place and looked at it steadfastly.

Sweet, child-like little face, clear, satisfied eyes, can you not speak to him, and tell him that love cannot die, that he is compassed about with a cloud of witnesses, that his struggles to live honestly, his despair at the revelation of his weakness, even his present sacrifice to a shadowy instinct rather than to a principle —all is helping to draw him towards you?

No, comfort cannot be his yet. He cannot see that the pain and loss are necessary to the great gain; he can only go on bravely and painfully in the darkness, holding to the faint track of right and duty which he begins faintly to perceive.

Presently the little cathedral clock was standing on a shelf among other clocks, large and small, in a Liverpool pawnbroker's shop, and Donovan was walking back to his room through the driving rain with head bent low, and thirty shillings in his pocket.

CHAPTER VII.

"O'ER MOOR AND FEN."

Self-reverence, self-knowledge, self-control,
These three alone lead life to sovereign power,
Yet not for power (power of herself
Would come uncall'd for), but to live by law,
Acting the law we live by without fear;
And, because right is right, to follow right
Were wisdom in the scorn of consequence.
                                        TENNYSON.

AND after all the struggle seemed utterly useless, for the Exeter —— Institute would not accept him as secretary. He was in every way suited for their purpose, and by far the most promising of the candidates; but in a close cross-examination the insuperable barrier was brought to light.

"And your religious views, sir?" asked the president. "As this is a charitable institution, we always make a point of knowing the views of our staff. It is well to be united. Do you belong to the High or Low party?"

"To neither," said Donovan, stiffly. "I am an atheist."

And in those four words lay his doom; because the institute was a *charitable* one it could not help such a hardened sinner, could not let its accounts and letters be contaminated by his touch.

"I have come from a great distance in the hope of getting this post," said Donovan, swallowing his pride. "I am very much in need of work. Surely in the mechanical work of a secretary such a matter as one's private creed might be passed over. What difference can it make to anyone else?"

"My dear sir," said the head of the charitable institution, "I can only refer you to the Bible, where you will find the injunction: 'Be not unequally yoked together with unbelievers,' and 'What part hath he that believeth with an infidel?'"

> "Alas! for the rarity
> Of Christian charity
> Under the sun."

With the indifference of his kind, however, the frigid adherence to the letter, and the disregard of the spirit, a sort of bitter resolution awoke in Donovan's heart. He would *not* be doomed by a "charitable" institution, he would *not* sink down quietly into starvation. Life in itself was not worth a straw, but just from opposition, from a manly love of breasting "the blows of circumstance," he would struggle on, fight down all obstacles, live to be of use too, in spite of the president's specimen of Christian generosity and brotherliness. Fiercely through his teeth he quoted Shylock's passionate words, "Hath not a Jew eyes? ... fed with the same food ... warmed and cooled by the same winter and summer as a Christian is?"

He had been two days at Exeter; now returning to his lodgings, he sat down and resolutely went over all possible plans for his future. Should he go back to Greyshot? Mr. Alleyne, the man with whom he used to read, might possibly put him in the way of employment. It was not very likely, though, and there were many objections to a return to the old neighbourhood. Should he write to old Mr. Hayes? He might be at home again by this time, though in the winter Doery had said he was still abroad. But Mr. Hayes was poor, and would unquestionably think only of monetary help.

No, that would not do. Should he go home and throw himself on his mother's mercy? But that thought was too wildly impracticable as well as too painful to be allowed for a moment. What connections had he in this part of the world? What had his father's business in Plymouth been, when four years ago they had gone there together? Searching back in his memory he at length recalled the name of his father's acquaintance, and remembered that he had described him as a pleasant elderly man. He was a banker—there would be no difficulty in finding his address.

He began a letter to him at once, a brief, business-like, stiff letter, not at all like that of a starving man asking for help. But then he had no intention of starving. He was young and strong-willed, undaunted still, notwithstanding his repulses.

Having despatched the letter, he made up his mind to follow it; there was no hope of finding work in this quiet old city; at Plymouth he would have more chance. He might just as well spend his time in getting there as in loafing about the Exeter streets. Getting there meant walking, for the proceeds of the clock were nearly exhausted, and would barely suffice to get him some sort of food and shelter, but he rather enjoyed the thought of the exercise, and even the prospect of " roughing it " a little.

So the next morning, with his few belongings stowed away in a small bag—the portmanteau had been discarded in Liverpool,—he set out on his walk. The natural energy of his character shone out strangely every now and then, in spite of the disastrous education which had so cramped it. No one meeting him that day, as he walked briskly along the Devonshire lanes, would have imagined that he was as poor as the veriest tramp, and had infinitely fewer resources than most beggars. His stern face was lighted up with resolute perseverance, there was a sparkle, not exactly of enjoyment, but of keen determination, in his eye; he held his head just as proudly as in the days when he had been Donovan Farrant, Esq., of Oakdene Manor.

It was a lovely July day, a little hot for walking certainly, especially in the deep lanes where every breath of air seemed to be shut out; but there was something satisfactory about the whole excursion, and Donovan walked on steadily. The high hedges were in their full beauty—beautiful as only Devonshire hedges can be, with their broad green fringes of hartstongues, their drooping lady ferns and sturdy bracken, their glorious wild roses and bramble bushes, with here and there a bit of mossy grey stone cropping out, or a miniature waterfall thrusting its silvery white head through the grasses, and tumbling with splash and splutter into the tiny wayside brook below. The smell of the new-mown hay gave a country fragrance to the air, and in most of the fields the men and women were hard at work, while wisps of sun-dried grass caught here and there on each side of the road proved that loaded waggons had already passed that way, leaving their trophies on the hedges.

Donovan had made up his mind to sleep at Chagford, and it was already late when he crossed Fingle Bridge. The view there was so exquisite, however, that he was obliged to stop for a few minutes; resting on the grey stone parapet, he looked down at the transparently clear river, along the green meadows and wooded valleys to the hills which, encircling all, stood out clearly defined against the soft evening sky. All was quiet and peaceful; in this country stillness and exquisite beauty, it seemed possible almost to realise that once all the world had been pronounced "very good." Donovan thought only, however, of the contrast of this peace with the world of competition, the overcrowded market of labourers in which he was trying to push his way. It was with a sigh that he turned away and walked on to the little grey town of Chagford, where the lights were beginning to shine out from the cottage windows, and the square tower of the church stood darkly above the lower roofs, a grim silent guardian.

Very early the next day he was on his way again, exulting in the fresh morning air, and greatly looking forward to the crossing of the moor. Waif scampered on in front, enjoying the exercise as much as his master, and Donovan found himself whistling as he walked. At length, leaving the cultivated region behind him, he struck across the wild waste of Dartmoor, and then the full delights of his walk came to him. The freshest, purest, strongest air in England was blowing in his face, his feet were treading a springy elastic soil, and all around him was a scene of the wildest beauty. The heather was not yet out, but the gorse blossoms still lingered, and made a golden glow over the great undulating expanse, while all round the tors raised their rugged, granite heads, now in full sunshine silvery white, now with a passing cloud shadow darkest purple—grotesque, fancifully shaped, irregular, and yet exactly harmonizing with the barren waste surrounding them.

On sped the dog and his master, now through marshy ground, springing from one tuft of heather to another, now up across the scattered granite blocks of a tor, and down again into a fresh featured waste on the other side, now startling a troop of the wild Dartmoor ponies which galloped away, their manes flying in the wind, and Waif barking at their heels, now stepping across one of the old British encampments with their imperishable "hut circles."

It was not till about five in the afternoon that he reached Prince Town, and then for the time his pleasure was clouded, for the first sight that greeted him was the great grey block of buildings where poor Noir Frewin had been unjustly immured. Passing some wretched little black cottages which are familiarly known as New London, he went down the hill to the town itself, on the way encountering a gang of convicts dragging a cart, and guarded by two warders, rifle in hand. The sight was a painful one, the men half patient, half sullen, looked at him curiously and envyingly; the warders urged them on.

Donovan had half thought of sleeping at Prince Town. He had been walking since seven o'clock that morning, and was rather tired, but the gloom of the place so oppressed him that he could not endure the thought of staying in it. He selected instead the cheapest-looking public house from the large number which the little place offered, had his dinner, and after a short rest prepared to go on again. The people of the house in vain tried to induce him to stay. He was not to be turned from his purpose, however, and having learnt that he could put up for the night at the "Dousland Barn Inn," if he went by the road, or at Sheepstor, if he went by the moor, he resolved to take the latter course.

By this time it was between six and seven in the evening, but he calculated that in even ordinary walking he should reach his destination before dusk, and with the bold outline of Sheepstor before him as a landmark, he steered his way across the waste. There was something awe-inspiring in the entire loneliness as he passed on further from Prince Town. Far and near not a creature, not a house was to be seen. Beauty, grandeur, even a faint shadow of the Infinite, who can fail to trace these in that glorious moor, unique in its wildness and expanse?

Involuntarily Donovan fell into a deep reverie. The purer nobler view of the world forced itself upon him; he had seen hitherto so little but the evil. And then naturally his thoughts went back to Dot, as they invariably did in his best moments, and he comforted himself in that terribly insufficient and yet pathetic way which Byron has expressed in one of his saddest poems.

> "The better days of life were ours;
> The worst can be but mine:
> The sun that cheers, the storm that lowers
> Shall never more be thine."

He had been walking on abstractedly; looking up at last, he was dismayed to find that a sudden mist had arisen, completely veiling the surrounding tors, and, what was worse, evidently spreading every minute. Here was a hindrance which he had never for a moment contemplated. The evening had seemed perfectly fine when he started; he had no compass, and had trusted implicitly to his eye in choosing the most direct route to Sheepstor. Now all traces of the tors were entirely obliterated.

It was not a very pleasant prospect. All manner of stories he had heard of travellers lost in the mist recurred to his memory; dismal tales of people who had wandered round and round in a circle for hours, never many yards distant from their starting-point, or of unfortunate pedestrians overcome by fatigue and cold. He stood still for a minute or two, called Waif to heel, and steadily faced the facts of the case. The mist was rolling nearer and nearer, hemming him in on every side; even now he could hardly see a yard in front of him! Although it was a July evening, the cold was enough to make him shiver; the mist pressed down on him impenetrably, every breath he drew brought him into closer contact with the heavy, damp, chill fog. Standing still was out of the question; he resolved to go on. Sheepstor lay, he thought, rather to his left, and as he had heard that the natural instinct in walking was to tend towards the right, he took a very decided course in the opposite direction.

On and on he went, ceaselessly but almost hopelessly on. He was growing very tired, too; the mist hung heavily upon him, he could not see an inch before his feet. Fearing that Waif might possibly stray, he had taken him up under his arm, and was plodding heavily along when he suddenly came to marshy ground. For three or four steps he floundered on, trying to regain the firm land, but what might have been done with sight, was simply impossible in the blinding mist. Another step, and he felt himself sinking deeper; a fierce struggle to free himself, and in a moment he was up to his knees in one of the treacherous Dartmoor bogs.

He uttered no invectives, but, when perfectly convinced of the hopelessness of struggling out, he drew Waif's head up so that he could look into the clear brown eyes.

"Waif, old boy," he said, "mother earth means to settle the question for us. Do you feel inclined to have done with your master, your bones, and biscuits, and wanderings?"

The dog, evidently understanding the danger, set up a howl so wildly piteous that Donovan's heart was touched.

"Poor old fellow, you'd rather go on, would you?"

And for a moment they looked full into each other's eyes with the strange comprehension that comes between some dogs and some men. Then Waif licked his master's face, and Donovan, all the time feeling that he was gradually sinking deeper, patted the white and tan head.

"Very well. Waif, as you say we'll have a try, take my hat, old boy," and he put his soft cloth hat into the dog's mouth, " scrunch it up, never mind! a hundred to one I shall never want it again! find a man if you can and bring him back here, do you understand? now go. There!" and with some effort he threw the dog as far from him as possible, and Waif, alighting where his trifling weight might be borne, tore off like the wind with the hat between his teeth.

In throwing the dog Donovan felt the soft ground beneath him sink considerably, an irresistible force sucked him down lower and lower, very soon he was up to his waist in the cold wet mud. Then he spread out both his arms and waited quietly for the end—whichever end it was to be.

He felt strangely indifferent. If death did come to him, why, then it would be well ; if he was rescued, there would be the satisfaction of not being conquered by the affection of good mother earth, who, having dealt rather coldly with him all the days of his life, now seemed determined to hold him in a clinging embrace.

His jacket was not fastened, he could see three buttons of his waistcoat. With a sort of grim sense of the ludicrous he resolved to use them as a measuring gauge, by which he could judge how fast he was sinking. It was bitterly cold down in this wet slush, on the whole he rather looked forward to the end. What was that odd recollection that came to him? He was a little child again, and Doery's prim face rose before him.

"Asleep in church, Master Donovan! oh! for shame! I wonder you wasn't afraid you'd never open your eyes in this world again."

And in spite of his strange position, even now, he could not help laughing as he recalled his childish sense of discomfort, and how for several Sundays after that he had not been able to let his eyelids drop in peace.

The first button disappeared.

Then he wandered on to recollections of his life with the Frewins, how they would wonder what had become of him! He was back in Drury Lane with Sweepstakes abusing him. He was in a railway carriage, and Noir was waving the cards before his eyes in the three card trick. He was sitting in the park and a bright-faced girl near him was talking of home, the sort of home which he had never been able to realise.

The second button disappeared.

Then he felt a strange impression of having been through this scene before, of having felt the cold wall of mist hemming him in, and after a time he remembered it had been in his nightmare about Dot. And over and over the words rang in his ears:

> "The better days of life were ours;
> The worst can be but mine."

"You are safe, Dot, my darling. ''Tis nothing that I loved so well,' I would not have you back even to the days that were ours. And the worst may be over for me, Dot, ended here out on Dartmoor!"

The third button disappeared.

"I wish I had not gone to that billiard-room," he mused, "I wish I could have died satisfied at least that my will was as strong as I used to think it. To fail! how hateful it is to fail! If I thought that I could get on, and not come to grief again so weakly, I should almost wish to get out of this bog and have another try."

The mist had now rolled away, but it was almost dark and the stars were shining above him. The night wind blew through his hair, waved the cotton grass growing around him, sighed and moaned over the desolate country. Nature sang him her dreariest death-song. Ah, well! death could not be more dreary than his life had been!

By this time he was up to his shoulders, and was obliged to raise his arms, the grass and rushes blew against his face. It was exceedingly unlikely that Waif would find help. In a very short time he must inevitably die. What a strange ending to his stormy life! strange and yet perhaps not inappropriate, to die here alone in the darkness, as he had lived, the grandeur and beauty and majesty of the great moor close to him, all around, but shrouded in the black night; faint imperfect images of the beautiful tors presented to him now and then, but never a true idea of their form.

By-and-by came a light, flickering wavering far in the distance. Was it a Will o' the wisp? Could he hold out any longer? Could he keep rigidly motionless till this possible help should reach him? A sort of dogged endurance and hatred of yielding came to renew his failing powers, his voice clear and strong rang out into the night. Yet why did he call? why did he not yield, and sink down quietly into nothingness? For an instant life and death, the chances of each, hung in a perfectly even balance, and his indifference turned to a decided wish for the end of the struggle. Should he call again? he thought not. But just as he was making his final resolution to keep the silence which would inevitably lead to death, he heard Waif's sharp anxious bark from afar.

"My dog, I won't be such a selfish brute," he exclaimed, realising Waif's faithful devotion, and thinking of his despair if the search should be of no use. "Ho! here! help!" and then, with his usual whistle, he tried to attract the dog's notice.

In a few minutes Waif was close to him, whining with delight, snorting with impatience, and tearing madly backwards and forwards between the approaching lantern and his submerged master. Then the bearer of the lantern came into view, a sturdy Devonshire farmer, and his almost equally sturdy son. Donovan hailed them eagerly.

"Veth!" exclaimed the farmer, "stogg'd in Foxtor Mire that ye are!"

"Set fast here for hours," said Donovan.

"No tanny bye! *(don't tell me!)*" exclaimed the good man, much shocked. "But we'd best talk when the deed's dune. The missus she says to me, 'maister, you take the laistest bit o' rope with ye, likely it's a bog accident.' So lay ye hold, my man, fast hold o' the end, and veth! we'll sune have ye safe and dry. Hold on, my man, and sure as my name's John Peek we'll have ye safe."

Then, with a tremendous effort, the sturdy Devonshire men pulled at the rope till Donovan's shoulders were free once more. After that they hastily threw a noose round him, and with infinite difficulty succeeded at length in dragging him from his slimy grave.

In a few minutes Donovan, encrusted in black mud, and so stiff and weary that he could hardly drag himself along, was safely on terra firma once more, and Waif, proud and happy, was springing about his feet.

Partly from physical causes, and partly from his sudden removal from the near contemplation of death, he fell into a half dreamy state, was not sure whether the sturdy farmer and his son were not after all shadows, even doubted whether Waif was not an illusion, while every weary step he took seemed to add to his strange indifference as to what was to become of him. If left to himself he would have plodded on and on till he dropped.

But John Peek was at his elbow—he was too muddy to be touched—piloting him across the moor in the direction of the farm, talking in his half unintelligible Devonshire dialect, and at length leading him through the yard gate, across the roughly-paved granite road to the little white farm house where he lived. At the sound of their footsteps the wife hastened out, a comely Devonshire woman, her short skirt, crossed neckerchief, smooth hair, and healthy-looking face, all as fresh and neat as could be. The husband explained matters, and Donovan was hurried into the kitchen, where, what with the warmth of the peat fire, the contrast between his horrible state of filth and the exquisite cleanliness of the place, added to the extreme difficulty of understanding the dialect of the farmer and his wife, he gradually came to himself, realised that he was actually alive, that his surroundings were no shadowy phantoms of the imagination, that he was still Donovan Farrant, possessed of little but a dog and a will which had failed, and with a blank future beyond, in which his primary object must be—not to starve.

In the immediate present, however, his only wish was to be clean once more, and with some difficulty he made himself understood. Evidently the farmer's wife thought cleanliness next to godliness, and fully sympathised with the desire.

"Zich a jakes *(such a mess)* as never was seen, fit to make my flesh crip, ess fay it is! Come ye up, zur, come ye up over the stairs," and the good woman led the way up the spotless staircase to a room above, where, with much ado, she brought a huge wooden washing tub, hot water, an enormous piece of soap, even a scrubbing-brush, crowning all her favours by fetching him an entire set of her husband's clothes!

Cincinnatus handled the plough, and doubtless wore the equivalent for fustian. History does not relate how he looked in rustic guise, but Donovan, with his "Roman" face and unmistakeable air of refinement, presented a very comical appearance in Farmer Peek's marketing costume. But the comfort of being dry and clean again was great, and he joined the farmer and his family in the kitchen, feeling able to speak the thanks for his rescue which till now had remained unsaid.

"And now zet down, zur, zet down, for ye luke mortal vagg'd," said the farmer, drawing up one of the Windsor chairs to the hearth. "Likely ye had a gude walk before ye got stogg'd i' the mire?"

"Yes, from Chagford," said Donovan, stretching his feet out to the smouldering peats.

"No, tanny bye! on the trat the whole blessed day!" exclaimed the wife, "and ye luke crewel tender."

He laughed and disclaimed any "tenderness."

"Zich walks isn't for the likes of ye," said the farmer, with a shrewd look at the wearer of his market-day suit; "ye should lave it to us pewer folk—it's not for gintry and passons."

Donovan could not help smiling at finding himself classed with parsons.

"I am poor," he said—"a tramp."

"Aw!" exclaimed the farmer, shaking his head with a knowing smile, "ye won't make us belave that, zur—no, no, us knows the gintry when we zee 'em."

"In spite of which, I am poor and a tramp,"

said Donovan; "and what few things I had left went down into Foxtor Mire."

"Ah, gude heaven!" exclaimed the wife, "it was a mercy ye didn't go yurself; but what will ye plase to take for zupper, zur? there's cream i' the dairy, and——"

"Whatever you would have for yourselves, nothing else," said Donovan.

The woman hesitated; he spoke as if he meant to be obeyed, but her hospitable soul longed to set the best things in the house before the hero of the evening.

"Veth, zur, it's not fitty for zich as ye," she began, but Donovan interrupted her.

"Nothing else, thank you," and his tone, more than the actual words, convinced the good woman that nothing but the usual supper must be prepared.

So Donovan sat down with the farmer and his wife to broth and "kettle-bread," and then, at his own request, was allowed to establish himself for the night before the fire; for, in spite of the summer evening, he had been so thoroughly chilled that he was glad of the warmth.

Before long all was quiet in the house;

Donovan, with Waif at his feet, lay very still but very much awake in the little kitchen. By this time all might have been over for him —how strange was the thought! He might have entered on the " peace of nothingness;" life might have been over, perplexities solved by the great silence, no trace of him left even, to carry sorrow to his mother or remorse to Ellis; and instead of this, he was still in the world, lying on his back moralising by the light of a peat fire!

It was a curious accident which had brought him like this under a hospitable roof; he had been in many odd places, but never in quite such a homely place as this. Half dreamily he let his eyes wander round the white-washed walls; opposite him was the tall eight-day clock, and a large copper warming-pan reflecting the dull red glow of the fire; above the high mantelshelf two rather ancient-looking guns, and a great array of tin pots and platters; below, a spotless white dimity frill hanging over the wide hearth; overhead, in the black rafters, hung sundry hams.

His own clothes were hanging up to dry as near the peats as the farmer's wife would allow, and glancing from them to the borrowed garments he wore, and for the first time realising that Farmer Peek was at least six inches shorter and immeasurably stouter than himself, that the fustian clothes hung about him in folds, and that his whole appearance was most utterly grotesque, he burst out laughing—laughed till the wooden rafters rang, till Waif started up and began to wag his tail sympathetically, till inevitably he would have roused the farmer and his wife, had they not slept as soundly as the Seven Sleepers. Certainly the personal danger he had been in had not awed him as a moralist might have desired; he went to sleep with nothing more sober in his thoughts than a verse out of Dot's " Nonsense Book "—

> "There was an old man of the West
> Who wore a pale plum-coloured vest;
> When they asked—does it fit?
> He replied, not a bit,
> That funny old man of the West."

The next morning came the rather humiliating necessity of explaining to the farmer his utter inability to reward him for his rescue and his hospitality. He was received, however, with all the delightful warm-heartedness and real courtesy so general in the west country.

"Aw! zur, ye didn't think a wanted money!

It's treu us a given ye the laistest bit of a help, but God bless ye, zur, us has been plased to du it."

"When I get on in the world, I shall not forget you, Mr. Peek," said Donovan, with firm confidence in the "when." "All I can do now is to thank you very much for your hospitality."

"Veth, zur, you're welcome. Us wull be plased to zee ye again, and I wish ye weel in zaking zarvice."

"Seeking service!" Donovan smiled, but the expression was true enough. He wished his worthy host good-bye, managed to leave his last coin—half-a-crown—in the market-day coat, and set off briskly on his fourteen mile walk to Plymouth.

Skirting round the foot of Sheepstor, he was soon on the road, with the bold outlines of Sharpitor and Leathertor on one hand, and far in the distance a line of silvery brightness where the sunlight fell on the sea. Life felt good. On the whole, he felt really glad that the blue vault was above him, not the black mud of the bog. Towards the afternoon, however, when he had been walking some hours, his spirits sank. The heat tried him a good deal; he began to feel very stiff and tired, as well he might after his adventure of the previous evening. And with the physical exhaustion came a degree less of confidence in the future. What if his father's acquaintance, Mr. X——, refused to help him? What if he could find no employment now? He walked on heavily, but still with resolution—come ill or well, he was ready to face it manfully, but his cheerfulness disappeared, and it was a stern-faced and very oddly-dressed candidate who presented himself at the door of the bank, and asked to see Mr. X——, the manager.

The bank was closed, but one of the clerks appeared in answer to his ring, and directed him to the manager's private house. He went there, and, with the bearing of a proud man forced to ask a favour, was shown into Mr. X——'s library.

A handsome keen-faced gentleman of about five and thirty was sitting at the table writing. He glanced up as Donovan was announced, scanned him from head to foot without rising, then bowed stiffly. This was Donovan's view.

Mr. X——, on the other hand, saw before him a tall, gaunt, handsome fellow, apparently about five and twenty, in clothes which were stained and shrunk to such a degree that a tramp would scarcely have said "thank you" for them, holding a ragged cloth hat in his hand, and in spite of his beggarly array, carrying his head very high. Such a shabby-looking fellow as this could hardly be asked to sit down on one of Mr. X——'s new red-morocco chairs. The good farmer's wife had carefully dusted the Windsor chair for him the night before, the banker was not so courteous or so well-bred. Throughout the interview Donovan stood.

The banker briefly asked his business. It appeared that the elder Mr. X—— had died two years before; the present one had never heard of Colonel Farrant. And then, after a few mutual explanations, Mr. X——'s rather quick peremptory manner became a little more suave as he said,

"You must, I think, see, Mr. Farrant, that your claims upon me are of the very slightest. Our respective fathers knew each other—at least, you tell me so. Even should I take you at your word without seeking to prove this to be the fact, however, it is hardly sufficient ground for—in short, you understand me, I am sure. I need not explain myself further."

"I understand perfectly," said Donovan, coldly. "You think I am come to beg. I am quite aware that I look like a beggar, thanks to one of your Devonshire bogs; but nothing is further from my thoughts. You were the only person I knew in the neighbourhood. I want work, and thought you might be able to advise me where to try for it."

"I am afraid, Mr. Farrant, you are a novice in these matters," said the banker. "One cannot at a moment's notice cause situations to spring up ready to hand; besides, in the letter I received from you from Exeter, you gave me no particulars and no references."

"I have none to give," said Donovan, shortly.

"You can at least tell me what your previous employment has been."

"I have only just returned from the Continent."

The banker looked at him a little curiously.

"And before that?"

Donovan coloured slightly, but answered, firmly,

"Before that I was a card-sharper."

The banker started.

"Bless me! and after this you expect me to patronise you, Mr. Farrant?"

"On the contrary," said Donovan, quietly, "I see plainly that that is the last thing you will do."

There was irony in the tone; the banker smiled a little, looked again at his strange visitor, and saw that, in spite of the beggarly array, he was evidently a clever fellow. He liked clever fellows, and his next remark sounded much more cordial; but Donovan's sensitive pride at once recoiled from the slight touch of vulgarity.

"I see you're sharp enough, Mr. Farrant, no lack of brains; but even if I knew of any situation likely to suit you, what guarantee should I have that you might not prove a little *too* sharp again?"

"No guarantee," said Donovan, wincing. "But I should hardly have answered your question with such perfect openness, if I had been the knave you take me for. I can give you no guarantee but my honour."

"And in business that would hardly answer," said Mr. X——, with a sharp-edged smile; "besides, the honour of an ex——"

"Good afternoon," said Donovan, moving to the door.

"Stay, stay," said the banker; "that was

rather hard lines. I can't help you to a situation, Mr. Farrant, but you seem in a very bad way, and as I see you're a clever fellow I will break through my ordinary rule. Day and Martin made their fortunes by giving away a stray sovereign, and, though I can hardly hope to do that, I have still great pleasure in giving you some small assistance."

He fumbled in his pocket, produced a gold coin, and pressed it into his visitor's hand.

There are some deeds of so-called "charity" which wound more deeply than actual unkindness, some favours which are more hard to endure than blows, some ways of giving so utterly intolerable to the recipient that even in need they must be rejected.

Donovan was actually penniless, he felt stiff, weary, ill, and already very hungry, but no power on earth could have brought him to accept the banker's tactless, ill-bred offer. He put down the sovereign, bowed, and hurried out of the house.

For a time indignation and those heart-stirrings which follow after an insult has been received kept him up; he tramped up and down the Hoe physically strong again because of the inward tumult of feeling. Then he wandered into the town, lounged wearily about the streets,

"Homeless near a thousand homes,"

and worse than homeless, utterly destitute in every way, sick at heart, ashamed of his past, miserable in the present, and hopeless as to the future.

When St. Andrew's clock struck nine, he was standing at the corner of the churchyard idly watching the passers-by, wishing that night would come that he might hide himself in the darkness and forget his weariness in sleep. But as time passed he grew more and more uneasy, and the dread of illness began to haunt him painfully; he had certainly eaten nothing since early morning, but that was not sufficient to account for the growing faintness which was stealing over him. He had had a dim idea of enlisting, but that faded away now, he was too wretched to wish for anything but shelter for the night, precisely the thing he had not.

There were only three alternatives, either he must break his resolution again and trust to his customary skill and good fortune, or he must try to sell Waif, or he must adopt the beggar's shelter—an arch or a doorway.

A sharp struggle was needed to dismiss the

first idea, the merest glance at the dog to prove the second impossible; then in pain and great weariness he wandered on once more. Only a month or two before he had had more money than he knew what to do with—it was strange to look back to the old life, with its excitement and success, and self-indulgence—and now, through his own doing, he was utterly cut off from it all. But he knew that it was well, and in a larger sense than before the words which had haunted him on Dartmoor came to him now,

"The worst can be but mine."

Failure, pain, ruin, starvation, all these were apparently his destiny; he felt that they were endurable because they involved no harm to others; it had been a choice of life and pleasure at the expense of his honour and his fellow-men, and death and suffering affecting himself alone. His contact with the world had changed his views greatly; a year ago he had been a misanthrope, now he saw the position of self and others inverted.

More than four years had gone by since the grave-looking Indian colonel and his son had passed up the steps of the Royal Hotel. Donovan, fresh from his school disgrace, full of hurt pride and bitter resentment of the injustice, had spent no very comfortable night there. Unlikely as it may seem, he slept a great deal better beneath the porch of one of the neighbouring houses than he had done before in the luxurious room. With Waif crouched up as near him as possible for the sake of warmth, with the cold night wind blowing on him, he slept well; in the old times he had been his own slave, now he was "lord of himself." Disheartened, humbled, with widened sympathies and self thrust low, he was now, in spite of the verdict of the president, a truer follower of Christ than some professing Christians, the only difference being that he followed bravely and painfully in the darkness, not even knowing his goal, while many of them in their full light follow sleepily and lazily, attaining to little of the broad-hearted love and self-abnegation to which they have pledged themselves.

Donovan did not dream, he was too completely worn out; his sleep was heavy and unbroken; but he woke early the next morning with a name in his mind—Porthkerran. What brought it there he could not tell. In thinking over his acquaintance in the West at Exeter, he had naturally remembered the Tremains; but it seemed utterly improbable that a doctor in a remote Cornish village would be able to help him to work, and he had never thought even of applying to him. But now, in the freshness of the July day, as he dragged himself up from his resting-place, and felt the utter impossibility of seeking work in his present state, the thought of Porthkerran, of the kindly doctor, of Mrs. Tremain, came to him as a light in his darkness. He was at that stage of illness when pride—even the pride of independence—is brought low, and though he had rejected the banker's sovereign but a few hours before, the idea of going to the Tremains and asking their help did not seem hard to him.

The only question was, should he ever get there? To loiter about in Plymouth in search of work would be both useless and impossible; but with an actual goal, a definite thing to be done, it was different. He made up his mind to go, and set off on the long walk patiently and deliberately, though anyone with a degree less of courage and resolution would have succumbed at once.

When he had walked about five or six miles the full difficulties of his undertaking came to him. On first waking he had felt ill indeed, but the sleep had to some extent refreshed him, and it was not till later in the morning that the unknown pains of hunger beset him. Still he toiled on, always on, with aching head and failing limbs, while above the summer sun blazed down on him in fullest power. What if the Tremains were no longer at Porthkerran? What if they turned him away because of his previous life, or his religious views? These were his only thoughts as he struggled on. By-and-by came faintness, and he was obliged to stagger to the side of the road and lie down on the grass, and then he lost count of time, and was very dimly aware that the intolerable heat and glare changed to cloudy coolness; it was not till a heavy shower of rain began that he came fully to himself, staggered to his feet once more, and resumed his walk.

For more than an hour the rain fell ceaselessly; when it stopped, he was soaked to the skin and very cold; even when the sun came out once more he was shivering from head to foot. How much farther could he manage? A sign-post, with "Porthkerran three miles," rather comforted him; he must and would get there, and once more he forced himself to go forward.

The road lay now along the cliffs overlooking

the deep blue sea. Donovan scarcely noticed anything, however, and it was not till the ringing clang of metal fell upon his ear that he looked up. By the side of the road was a blacksmith's forge; the blazing fire looked tempting; he entered the shed, and asked leave to warm himself.

The smith, a fine-looking man, with thick black hair tinged with grey, and eyes of deep blue like the Cornish seas, turned round quickly on hearing himself addressed.

"Come in, friend, and welcome."

The voice was a hearty one, but the smith was busy, and turned to his hammer and anvil once more, while Donovan drew near to the fire, and felt a little temporary relief from the warmth.

Presently wheels were heard, and a carriage stopped at the door; the smith put down his hammer and stepped briskly forward.

"Well, doctor—gude day to you—cast his shue, has he?"

Donovan heard the words distinctly, but they conveyed no meaning to his mind; he stared down vacantly into the glowing furnace, not even turning his head to see either the horse or the driver. A man's voice was explaining.

"Half a mile back, Trevethan. How long will you take to put him on a fresh one? I'm in a hurry to be at Mr. Penruddock's."

"Slow and sure, doctor—not less nor a quarter hour, and maybe more."

"Why don't you walk to the Penruddocks', papa? I can hold Star, and Ajax is so quiet there'll be no fear of his doing any harm."

It was a girl's mellow voice speaking—a voice in which there lurked laughter, tenderness, and yet a quaint sort of dignity. Donovan recognised it in a moment, and with a sudden return of strength and energy hurried to the door.

CHAPTER VIII.

ONE AND ALL.

Deal meekly, gently, with the hopes that guide
The lowliest brother straying from thy side;
If right, they bid thee tremble for thine own,
If wrong, the verdict is for God alone.

. . . .

Strive with the wanderer from the better path,
Bearing thy message meekly, not in wrath;
Weep for the frail that err, the weak that fall,
Have thine own faith, but hope and pray for all.
     OLIVER WENDELL HOLMES.

ONE glance at the little group without told him everything. There was the smith scrutinizing Star's shoeless foot; standing beside the other pony was Dr. Tremain himself, a little greyer than he had been four years ago, but not much altered; and in the pony-carriage sat Donovan's ideal, whom he knew now to be Miss Tremain—Gladys Tremain—for the unusual name recurred to his memory with the thought of the evening when he had first seen her in her own home, had heard her singing words which had moved him strangely.

With this sudden revelation, all thought of his present state of need passed from his mind; he only felt that he must do something for her, and with a word to the smith he went to Star's head.

"Ah! that'll du, doctor; now ye can go up to Squire Penruddock's; here's a chap as'll hold the pony steady."

Instinctively Donovan kept his face turned from Dr. Tremain; he could not bear to risk being recognised just then. The doctor saw only a tall figure in very shabby clothes—some friend of Trevethan's, he supposed; he merely glanced at him, told Gladys to drive on to meet him when the pony was shod, and walked away in the direction from which Donovan had just come.

The wind had risen, a west wind, and it blew strongly, though not coldly. Donovan could see the ribbons on Gladys' hat fluttering, though, after the first, he did not directly look at her, but kept his face half hidden. He could hear her talking to Trevethan, and once or twice some antic of Star's made her laugh.

She was evidently a favourite with the blacksmith; Donovan could see how the man's blue eyes lit up when she spoke to him.

Gladys, meanwhile, looked curiously at the motionless figure at Star's head. She had seen him as he came out of the shed, but for such a moment that she had only caught a sort of vision of a very pale, worn face. Who could he be? Some one whom Trevethan knew, or merely a tramp? Yet his attire was scarcely like a tramp's; shrunk, and stained, and dirty as it was, it had a look of better days about it. Who was he? She wished he had not been quite so near, for it was impossible to ask the blacksmith any questions about him. Ought she to give him something for holding the pony? Looking at him again, she was sure that he was visibly shivering, and that decided her. She opened her purse, and took out a sixpence. He looked ill, and cold, and very poor. He had been very good in holding Star; assuredly he ought to have something.

All this time she had only seen his back. When the shoeing was finished, and Trevethan had been paid, she drew up the reins, and rather shyly said, "Thank you for your help," holding out the coin to him as she spoke.

Oddly, though she had been rather curious to see his face, in putting the sixpence into his hand she looked at that; then, startled to find a smooth white palm instead of a hand roughened by hard work, she looked up quickly and saw a face which seemed partly familiar to her, a face with chiselled features, and dark cavernous eyes with a look of pain in them. But even as she first glanced at him his lips smiled slightly; he raised his hat.

"Oh! I beg your pardon. I did not see," she stammered, looking at the slender fingers which had closed over her sixpence, and colouring crimson.

"Thank you," he replied, in a tone which she could not mistake for sarcasm. "I am very much obliged to you."

Then he raised his hat again, and turned away; and Gladys drove off with hot cheeks. Where *had* she seen him before?

Donovan went back to the forge, partly for the sake of warming himself, partly in the hope of learning something about the Tremains. The blacksmith was busy, however, and he could only elicit the information that " that was their doctor up to Porthkerran, and a rale gude one he was;" that " Miss Gladys did gude to everyone she spoke to, and was like a bit of God's sunshine, and no mistake," with a few other most patent and obvious facts. Then, all the time swinging his great hammer, Trevethan began singing one of Wesley's hymns, and before he had come to the end, the pony-carriage passed the door once more.

"Will the doctor be going home now?" asked Donovan, as soon as he could make himself heard.

"Yes, belike," said the blacksmith, pausing in his work, and looking at his companion. "You'd du weel, friend, to go and see him, for you look mortal vagg'd. If you're passin' this way again, come and take your tae with me. You shall have a gude welcome."

"Thank you," said Donovan, touched by the off-hand yet real hospitality.

Then Trevethan having directed him to the doctor's house, which he already knew well enough, he set off once more.

Before he had gone far, a turn in the road brought him in sight of the Tremains' pony-carriage. It was standing still. Drawing nearer, he saw Gladys standing, bare-headed, on the verge of the cliff, her sunny hair blowing about in the wind. She seemed to be searching for something. Dr. Tremain, holding the reins at arm's length, was also peering down.

"Better give it up, my dear," Donovan heard him say. "We couldn't reach it, even if we could see it."

"Can I be of any use?" asked Donovan, coming towards the two. "Is anything lost?"

"My hat," said Gladys, turning round, but colouring as she saw who the speaker was.

Donovan's quick eyes were soon scanning every nook and cranny of the rugged cliff, and, after a minute's steady progress up and down, he detected far below a tiny moving speck, which he pronounced to be an end of ribbon.

"Will you allow me to fetch it for you?" he asked, forgetting his weakness and weariness in his desire to serve her.

"Oh! no, it is so far down," she said, quickly. "It is not the least worth while."

But Donovan was not to be deterred from the errand by its difficulty, and disregarding Dr. Tremain's remonstrances, he began to clamber down the cliff in a way which showed that he was either well used to the Cornish coast, or else an expert gymnast.

"He held Star just now at the forge," said Gladys to her father. "And I am sure I have seen him before, papa. Who can he be?"

The doctor was too intent on watching the descent, however, to answer, and when he did speak it was only to exclaim,

"Well done! he's got it." And then to criticise his way of setting about the ascent. "Quite right, he means to keep to the left, and skirt round that great boulder; bravo! that was cleverly managed. Come, Gladys, after this you'll have to make a speech. It's really very good of this young fellow. Hullo! though, he's slipped."

For Donovan had trusted to an insecure foothold, and had slipped down about six feet. Gladys gave a little cry, but happily a projecting boulder prevented any danger of a serious fall, and the two watchers saw that at least their helper was in no immediate peril. He was quite still, though; that began to frighten them.

"Are you hurt?" shouted the doctor.

But no answer came, and the figure still remained crouched up in the same position. Dr. Tremain felt very uneasy, but in two or three minutes Gladys gave a relieved exclamation.

"See, papa, he moves, he is getting up again."

They could see the tall figure struggling up,

indeed, but the doctor saw at once that something was wrong.

"Are you hurt?" he shouted once more.

"Yes," came back the answer, "but I'll manage it in a minute."

He had fallen with his ankle twisted under him, and had given it a sprain; it was indeed a very awkward situation, for the cliff was steep and hard to climb, and now, with the acute pain he was suffering, it seemed almost impossible; he looked at the little white hat hanging on his arm, and he looked up the grey cliff to Gladys. After all it only needed patience and a resolute disregard of the pain—he would try it. But it was infinitely harder than he expected, over and over again he turned dizzy, and was obliged to pause, and at last each step became a perfect battle. He could not attempt to answer the questions which reached him from above, every power was strained to its utmost in the physical struggle, in the conflict between the resolutely persevering "I will," and the overwhelming pain and weakness and difficulty.

At length, with an almost superhuman effort, he dragged himself up to the top, grasped the doctor's outstretched hands, crawled on to the smooth grassy plateau bordering the cliff, and, without a word, sank down prone, while Waif, with low whines, walked round and round him in great distress. Large drops of perspiration stood on his forehead, yet his face expressed little but hard fixed resoluteness, the iron will leaving its tokens even in semi-consciousness. The doctor looked at him intently for a moment, then he raised him so that his head rested on Gladys' knee, and prepared to examine his ankle. The merest touch caused a sharp thrill of pain, and Donovan opened his eyes.

"Oh! I am so very, very sorry," said poor Gladys. "I am afraid you have hurt yourself dreadfully."

"Only a sprain, I think," he answered, faintly, and then his eyes closed again.

"We must get him home as soon as possible," said the doctor. "I will bring up the pony-carriage as near as may be, and I think, Gladys, you had better run back to the forge and ask Trevethan to come and help. We shall be less likely to pain him if there are two of us to lift him in."

The doctor went to see to the pony-chaise, and Gladys was just going to obey him, when she was startled by a peremptory, "No, don't go," from the prostrate figure she was supporting. Then, to her dismay, he slowly raised himself and staggered towards the carriage.

"You should not have tried it," remonstrated the doctor, helping him in, and making him put up his foot at once on the opposite seat. "Now, Gladys, jump in quickly and drive us home. I shall sit here," and he established himself beside the injured ankle, holding it in a way which lessened the jar of the wheels.

The last exertion had proved too much even for Donovan's strength, however; he was only dimly conscious now, just realising from the pain that he was being driven somewhere, where he neither knew nor cared, or whether this half dream of incessant motion and incessant pain went on for ever and ever. All seemed a matter of supreme indifference. When the carriage at last stopped he felt no curiosity as to what was to follow, and, after a few minutes' pause, submitted without a word to being lifted out and borne *somewhere*, never once raising his eyelids to see what they were doing with him. Presently he became aware that his boot was being cut, and then came an instant's sharp pain, and he fainted.

Everyone who has experienced it knows the

extreme discomfort of a return to consciousness. Donovan came to quickly, however, partly aided by an odd association. The very first thing he distinguished was the smell of brandy, then he felt a glass held to his lips. From sheer annoyance he gained strength to push it away, and in weak, but decidedly cross tones, said quickly,

"Get away with your abomination, Rouge; I tell you I won't touch it!"

"Don't trouble him, he's coming to," said the doctor, and then Donovan, fully roused by the words, half raised himself and looked round.

"I beg your pardon," he said to the doctor, "I thought I was with some one else."

"I am afraid I hurt you a good deal just now; I ought to have seen you were getting faint and given you a restorative first," said Dr. Tremain.

"Faint!" cried Donovan, with all a man's dislike of making a scene. "You don't mean that I fainted."

"Certainly, the moment I touched your foot," said the doctor, smiling; "and, what is more, you will be fainting again before long if you don't take something. Try this," and he poured some milk into a tumbler and held it to his lips.

Donovan drank it and revived a little.

"It was not the pain," he said, abruptly, "I was half starved." Then glancing round the room, he continued in an odd, forced voice, "You shouldn't have brought me to your house; is there no workhouse or hospital at Porthkerran?"

"You shall consider this your hospital; I can promise you at least one resident doctor and several nurses," said Dr. Tremain, smiling.

"Don't laugh," said Donovan, "it is no laughing matter; I haven't a farthing in the world, I'm worse off than most beggars; couldn't you have seen by these that I wasn't fit for you to take in," and he touched his clothes.

"My dear fellow, do you think that makes any difference, or that we show our hospitality in Cornwall by shipping off our helpers to the workhouse? Come, don't talk nonsense, but tell me when you had your last meal."

"Yesterday morning between eight and nine."

"Whew!" the doctor gave a slight whistle, felt his patient's pulse again, and, turning to the servant, gave orders for some gruel to be made at once. When that had been administered, Donovan sank into a sort of doze. Presently he knew that a fresh voice was speaking, a low, pleasant voice. He came to that borderland of sleep when words begin to convey some meaning, the quiet mist-wreathed entrance to full consciousness.

"Has he got everything he wants?"

"Everything just now; he is simply worn out. Gladys has told you how we met him, I suppose."

"Yes, everything. I wish I had been at home when you came back. Is it a very bad sprain?"

"I daresay it wasn't at first, but imagine climbing up the cliff near the forge after he'd done it! There's good in that fellow, depend upon it; it was a spirited thing to do, especially in the state he was in. He owned he was half starved."

"Poor boy! I wonder how he happened to be in such straits."

Donovan began to show signs of waking; the voices ceased, but he felt a soft hand putting back the hair from his forehead; it reminded him of the feel of little Dot's tiny fingers, and then, with a rush of shame, he felt how unfit he was for such tenderness.

Suddenly opening his eyes, and half sitting up, he said, quickly,

"Look, you must get me moved in some way, I'm not fit to stay here."

Mrs. Tremain thought him feverish; but the doctor partly understood him.

"He is afraid of giving trouble; you must tell him there is nothing you like better than nursing."

"No," interrupted Donovan, "that is not it; listen to me, and then, if you will—turn me out; you won't be the first who has done so. I was once a card-sharper. I haven't a penny in the world. I am an atheist. Was I wrong in saying you would be wiser if you turned me out of doors?"

"Quite wrong," said the doctor, in an odd, quiet voice.

Then there was silence for a few minutes, and Donovan felt the soft woman's hand on his hair once more. For a moment he breathed hard, and there was a quiver in his voice when he said at last,

"I had given up expecting to be tolerated after that confession. I don't know why you are so different from other people. I might have guessed, though, that you would be. Mrs.

Tremain," he looked steadily up at her, "do you remember me?"

She gazed at him in perplexity, half remembering the face, and yet utterly unable to say where she had seen it. He raised his hand and pushed back the dark waves of hair from his forehead, revealing a long, white seam, the ineffaceable mark of his old wound. And with the sight there flashed back into Mrs. Tremain's mind a vision of the past.

"Mr. Farrant!" she exclaimed.

"Donovan Farrant—yes."

The doctor stood with an expression of surprise and great uneasiness on his face. If this were Donovan Farrant, how came it that he was a penniless adventurer? How came it that little more than a year after reaching majority he had come to Porthkerran in a state of semi-starvation? There must have been foul play somewhere. That will he had witnessed could not have been properly executed, or such a state of things could not have been. This evening, though, he must ask no questions, his patient was not fit for it. So he put away the uncomfortable thoughts as well as he could, and, coming forward, took Donovan's hand in his.

"I remember you very well now. I wonder I did not at first; but you are a good deal changed. We have often thought of you, and wondered whether you would ever come down to see Porthkerran again. I was glad to have you before I knew your name, and, knowing it, I am doubly glad. But now, as your doctor, I must forbid any more talking. Some more food first, and then you'd better settle in for the night."

"One thing more," said Donovan, "do you realise that there are two of us?" and he pointed to Waif. "He's all I have in the world. I can't part with him."

"Not even last night when you were starving?"

Donovan shook his head.

"Perhaps, though, I ought not to ask you to take him in, beggars can't be choosers."

"My dear fellow," said the doctor, laughing, and patting the dog's head, "will you never learn to believe that we are not utter brutes. Of course, the dog is welcome to spend the rest of his life here. I must quote the Cornish motto to you—'One and all.'"

With these words echoing in his ears, Donovan lay watching the busy preparations for the night which were being made by Mrs. Tremain and the servant. The room he had been carried to was on the ground floor, a school-room, he fancied, but now busy hands were converting it into a bed-room, and busy feet without were hurrying up and down the stairs, and along the passages, fetching and carrying. "One and all"—they were certainly carrying out their motto! And Donovan, who would have been sorely chafed by having to submit to a grudging service, watched his present nurses almost with pleasure. The comfort, too, of being in a home-like room again was very great. He ran through in his mind all the wretched places he had slept in, from the room in Drury Lane to his last night's shelter under a porch. Philosophically as he had endured them, it was, nevertheless, an unspeakable comfort to be again where all was fresh and clean, a relief, too, to be not in a mere living place, but a home. He read the titles of the books in the bookshelf, then glanced round the walls, half fearing to see once more his old enemy, the dingy oil-painting of the shipwreck. Instead, however, he found Wilkie's "Blind Man's Buff," next to that an elaborate chart of the kings of England, with illuminated shields and devices, which, no doubt, had been painted by Gladys; then a print of a "Holy Family," by Raphael, and lastly, just opposite him, Ary Scheffer's "Christ the Consoler."

He looked at this long and earnestly, struck by the great beauty of the idea it embodied, and, through the wakeful feverish night which followed, the vision of the face of Christ and the thought of the Cornish motto haunted him incessantly.

The next day, the doctor not being at all satisfied with his patient's state, and being besides anxious to learn the reasons of his poverty, induced him to speak of his past life.

"You are not nearly so strong-looking as when I saw you last," he began, drawing a chair up to the bedside. "Tell me what you have been doing with yourself, and then perhaps I shall understand your case better."

"It was four years ago that I saw you," replied Donovan. "It's likely enough I should be changed since then. Do you want the whole story?"

"As much as you feel inclined to tell," said Dr. Tremain. "Both as your friend and as your doctor I shall be glad to hear. After you left Porthkerran, you went to your home in Mountshire, I believe?"

"Yes," said Donovan, twisting a corner of the sheet as he spoke. "We went back to Oakdene, and after about two years my mother married again—she married the man who was my guardian, Ellis Farrant. He came to my father's funeral. I daresay you remember him."

Dr. Tremain tried not to show his dismay at this piece of news, and Donovan continued.

"He had always hated me, and there were constant quarrels between us; the final one would have come sooner if it had not been for my little sister. Partly for her sake I tried to behave decently to him. She died the winter before last. For a little while my step-father left me in peace, but directly I proposed entering some profession he told me I must expect nothing from him. That of course led to a quarrel, and in the end I was turned out upon the world to get on as best I could."

"But your father's will?" questioned Dr. Tremain, trying to speak quietly.

"He left all to my mother, unconditionally, and of course she could do nothing for me, even if she wished to."

The doctor sighed deeply, and there was a very troubled look on his face as he glanced at his patient.

"Poor fellow! you have been hardly used. Where did you go?"

"To London; but not one of our old friends would have a word to say to me, and I could get nothing to do. At last I fell in with a man named—well, never mind his name; he has been a good friend to me, even though he is a professional gambler. I went into partnership with him; it was impossible to live honestly, and I thought the other way would be bearable enough, for I was crazy at the injustice I had suffered, and hated everyone. But it didn't do. I found after a time I couldn't stand it. And then I went in for congestion of the lungs, that was last January. As soon as might be, I went abroad, but at Monaco had a relapse, which kept me back for another month. A little later, I found that I must break with my old friends and give up the sort of life I'd been living. I came back to England, and tried hard to find work, and by living cheaply, managed to spin out my money for a little while. I very nearly got a place as secretary at Exeter, but the man asked me point-blank what religious views I held, and that settled the question. I'd scarcely anything left then, but I made up my mind to come to Plymouth, and walked across Dartmoor. There I almost came to grief in a bog —it's a thousand pities I didn't quite—but Waif and a good Devonshire man hauled me out. The next day I came on to Plymouth, without a farthing, as I told you, and yesterday morning, being ill, either from the hours I spent in the bog, or from the unusual bed of stones, I felt only fit to crawl on to Porthkerran, hoping that you might help me."

It was evidently a relief to him when he had finished his story, and the doctor, who had been pleased with his brief straightforward confession on the previous night, was glad that he still kept to the mere outline of his life. He never alluded to those personal thoughts and details which go to make up the interest of any life-story, never attempted to excuse himself in any way, but, with some effort, just stated the main facts.

Dr. Tremain sat in silence for a few minutes. That Donovan had been cruelly wronged, he knew, and the mere fact of that would have given him a special claim upon his love and sympathy. But the thought of his life, his rebuffs, his temptations, his fall, his efforts to do right, appealed even more strongly to the doctor's heart. "I found I must give up the life I'd been living." What struggles, what absolute sacrifice lay within that one sentence!

While he was musing over what he had heard, Donovan watched him silently. Already the very deepest love for this man had sprung up in his heart—a strange, dependent love, which he had never before known—the love which, latent in all hearts, is usually awakened by the first true thought of God. A God-like deed, and the love shining in a man, had now touched into life this natural instinct, and Donovan, in his pain and humiliation, was yet all aglow with the strange new joy of devotion, enthusiasm, reverent admiration, the echo of the love first given.

The prolonged silence would have been hard to bear, if he had not had the most entire yet inexplicable faith in his new friend; but as it was he waited in perfect content. Presently the doctor looked up with great gladness in his face.

"Do you know I'm very glad you told me you were coming to us."

"Why?" asked Donovan, a little surprised

that this should be the only comment on his story.

"Because it shows that you've pluck enough to do what I fancy was very disagreeable to your pride."

"I don't know," said Donovan. "I suppose it was partly being so done up, but I didn't think about minding the asking a favour. I only felt need of you, and dread that I should never be able to get to Porthkerran."

"I can't imagine how you ever did get here," said the doctor, who knew that the walk would have been simply impossible to most people under the same circumstances. "I'm afraid you've been very rash in your self-management for some time past, and that is the reason you are suffering so much from your exposure. After two such illnesses as you described to me, a man needs some care for the next few months, at least. Did you take any care of yourself, or—mind, I only ask as a doctor—did you stay on at Monaco, ruining your health by excitement at the casino?"

"I only went to Monte Carlo once," replied Donovan, "and that before the relapse. Don't think it was any self-denial on my part; it was simply because I lost the first time, and because

I hated the other evils of a gambling place. For the rest I was quiet enough. Since I came to England, of course, I have lost ground."

"You have taken no care of yourself," said the doctor.

"Life isn't worth much extra fuss," said Donovan; "and besides, I was too poor. Short commons, no work, and intolerable dulness do pull a fellow down."

"Ah, yes; you must have felt dull when you gave up gaming," said the doctor, rather wishing to draw him out.

"Very," was the laconic answer. Then, as if remembering that he had no ordinary listener, he added—"It's only since then that I've had the least idea how weak one's will is. It certainly is humbling to find that after you've resolved to do a thing it needs a constant struggle not to give in after all."

"What made you first think of giving it up?" asked the doctor.

And Donovan then gave him an account of the miserable day in Paris, when M. Berrogain disappeared, and gradually Dr. Tremain realised how matters stood with his guest.

He came out of Donovan's room understanding him far better, yet feeling much more than he had yet done the great anxiety of his own position. This comparative stranger had peculiar claims upon him; he had been aware of that directly he had heard his name, but now, having heard the story of his life, he could not but feel what care and tenderness and wisdom were needed in dealing with such a character. Undoubtedly this great self-renunciation was a turning-point in Donovan's life, this awakening thought for others a sure sign of growth; what if by any ill-judged word or deed of his he should be thrown back or discouraged? The doctor was the most humble of men; greatly as he longed to help his guest, he trembled at the immense responsibility and difficulty, and grieved over his own unfitness for the task. For what was not required of him? Donovan was friendless—he must be his friend; cheated of his inheritance—he must, if possible, right him; burning with the sense of injustice—he must try to influence and soften him; and— most terrible thought of all—he believed in no God; some one must—— The doctor paused —nay, what? teach him—impossible! Argue with him?—probably useless; love him, pray, agonise for him—that he must and would do. The rest?

He was standing by the open door which led from the house into the garden; he saw the grand old cedar at the end of the lawn, standing up darkly against the clear sky, the acacia and the beech-trees waving in the wind, the standard roses laden with flowers, the glorious sunshine flooding all with warmth and brightness. He heard the singing of birds, the low hum of insects, the soft breathing of the summer wind among the branches. A sense of breadth and fulness stole over him, it was a healthful morning, and gradually Dr. Tremain felt its real influence, it drew him away from the thought of weakness and soul-disease to the true health-giver. Could he doubt that through all the changes and chances of Donovan's life He had been leading him? Then that strange and sudden impulse to walk to Porthkerran must have been part of the leading. The doctor accepted the responsibility gladly now, as a care doubtless, but as an honour and a joy. And as the free air and light and warmth influenced him from without, feeling that he lacked wisdom, he turned to Him who "giveth to all men liberally."

While he still stood in the doorway Gladys

came to him, her usually bright face a little clouded.

"Oh! I thought you had started on your rounds, papa," she exclaimed, brightening at once as she slipped her hand within his arm. "I've come to you in a very bad temper, for Aunt Margaret is here, and she is so much surprised at your taking in Mr. Farrant."

"Why is she surprised?" asked the doctor.

"Because you know so little of him. She thinks it most quixotic of you. I came away at last, she made me so cross."

"You and I believe in something better than chance, don't we, Gladys?" said the doctor. "And if Donovan Farrant was sent to us, as I do not doubt he was, our duty is to take care that we are fit to keep him with us."

"Fit?" asked Gladys, looking puzzled.

"Gentle and patient and considerate enough to draw him quite in amongst us, to make him part of the home. I will tell you a little about him, and then you'll understand me better. He has had a very sad life, he doesn't believe in God, partly, I can't help thinking, because he has never come across real Christianity. He has had great temptations, and no friends to help him, only companions whom at last he felt obliged to leave, that he might try to keep out of evil, and now he is here, ill and poor and I'm afraid very miserable. I know quite well that people will say, as Mrs. Causton has just been saying, that it is rash and quixotic to take him into one's own home, but, Gladys, I trust all of you too well not to look upon you as helps instead of hindrances."

"Do you know, papa, I have seen Mr. Farrant before," said Gladys, when her father paused. "I was sure I knew his face, and last night I remembered it was when I was staying with Aunt Margaret a year ago; don't you recollect that journey which auntie is always talking about, when we were in a carriage with some men playing cards?"

"I remember. There was only room for you, and one of them got out and gave his place to Mrs. Causton."

"Yes, that was Mr. Farrant."

The doctor mused. In his worst times, then, Donovan had kept a touch of chivalry, he had left his favourite pastime to save a stranger from a slight annoyance.

"We knew directly he was a gentleman,"

continued Gladys. "You can't think how different he looked from the men he was with. I couldn't think why he belonged to them, and one specially spoke so horridly to him at London Bridge, when we all got out, I fancy because he had helped us. Why was he ever with such people, papa?"

"Because no one else would have anything to do with him, and because he was a great card-player; he has given it all up now."

"Oh! I am so glad!" exclaimed Gladys, "for it was dreadful to watch him playing that day, he looked so wonderfully taken up with it, as if it were the only thing he cared for. It must have been very hard to him to give it up, though."

"Harder, most likely, than you or I have any idea of," said the doctor, musingly. Then, rousing himself, "And all this time we are leaving the mother to Mrs. Causton's tender mercies. I must go, little girl, good-bye. That story has smoothed your temper, I hope."

Gladys laughed, and ran away to give Jackie his morning lessons, while Dr. Tremain made his way to the breakfast-room.

He was not sorry to find Mrs. Causton on the

point of leaving, but unfortunately his appearance on the scene caused a repetition of all her arguments.

"And do you really think it wise to take him in and let him mix with your own children—a perfect stranger, a man of whom you know nothing but evil?"

"On the contrary," replied the doctor, half inclined to lose his temper, "I know a great deal of good about him."

"But it seems so unnecessary," urged Mrs. Causton; "no one in his circumstances could object to being taken to a hospital; and when he comes out, there are plenty of societies which would gladly take him in hand. There are so many societies for young men, you know."

"My dear Mrs. Causton"—the doctor spoke almost fiercely—"what the poor fellow wants is a *home*, not a society; he wants to be treated as a son, not as a case. I don't mean that societies are not useful enough sometimes, but I do think we are too ready to shunt on to them all that is not easy, self-indulgent, conventional charity. Look at the good Samaritan now—himself, by the way, an infidel and outcast—*he* did things all round; no passing on to committees and societies there, no holding at arm's length lest the poor fellow should stain his garments. He put himself to some inconvenience—perhaps to some risk, and gave the wounded man his own beast."

"Of course no one disputes that the parable is a great example," said Mrs. Causton, "an example that we should all copy; but still in this case——"

"You would have me enact the priest and Levite," interposed the doctor, "or pass on to some blundering committee for probing and examining and questioning a man who can scarcely bear to be touched. I know quite well that you would have most of the world on your side, for the good Samaritan style of giving is out of fashion now; we like to ride on in state and fling subscriptions here and there. We don't like the trouble or risk of actually dismounting and walking on foot; it isn't political economy."

"You may be right," said Mrs. Causton, half convinced; "and yet, for the sake of Gladys specially, is it wise and prudent? I don't want to seem intrusive, but one cannot help seeing that there are very grave objections to such an intimacy for her."

No one spoke for some minutes. This view

of the matter had certainly not occurred to Dr. Tremain, and he was bound to own that there was some truth in it. Was he putting his child into a wrong position? And yet could he, for the sake of a distant and merely possible contingency, give up his guest? His perplexity did not last long; he was not worldly-wise, he was not prudent, and, in defiance of the possible ill, he held closely to the present good, trusting to God, and feeling perfect confidence in Gladys. He had, moreover, with the strange insight of humility, learnt enough of Donovan's real self to trust in him too; the banker had exclaimed at the honour of an ex-card-sharper, the doctor felt inexplicable yet entire confidence in the truth of his patient.

"Some risk and trouble and difficulty I owned to in the Samaritan's giving," he said at last. "I do not think it a risk which one ought to shrink from. Were you ever in the Cluny Museum, Mrs. Causton?"

"Never."

"I remember two very striking representations there of Prudence with her hands tied, and Charity with open arms."

Mrs. Causton, not caring to discuss the question any more, soon took leave. The doctor was glad to be alone with his wife.

"You have not changed your mind?" he asked. "You are willing to be the open-armed Charity?"

"Yes," she replied, quietly, "I am willing." But there was some effort in her voice, for she thought of the possible sorrow which this charity might bring to Gladys.

"Then, having made up our minds, let us live in the present, and put away from us this idea, which I am half sorry has been suggested at all," said the doctor. "No one will put any nonsense into Gladys' head, and the friendship of a good sensible girl will be a capital thing for Donovan."

Mrs. Tremain looked up at her husband and smiled.

"How soon you have taken that poor boy into your heart of hearts! Oh! Tom, how far I am behind you; a dozen selfish considerations have come into my head in the last five minutes. I'm afraid I've little but pity for him."

"Then, dear, go and spend an hour in his room, and I'll undertake to say that he will stand second only to Dick and Jackie in your heart when you come out again."

CHAPTER IX.

IN A HOME.

It is human *character* or developed humanity . . . that conducts us to our notion of the Character Divine . . . In proportion as the mysteries of man's goodness unfold themselves to us, in that proportion do we obtain an insight into God's.
Essay on Blanco White. J. D. MOZLEY.

But the love slid into my soul like light.
Olrig Grange. WALTER C. SMITH.

DONOVAN looked up with a smile of welcome as Mrs. Tremain came into the room. He had been in too much pain to notice her much when she had visited him earlier in the morning, but now he was comparatively at ease, and was lying in listless quiet with Waif on the bed beside him licking his hand.

Mrs. Tremain was not fond of dogs; she was even a little afraid of them, and she had a very natural feminine dislike to seeing a fox terrier lying on a clean counterpane. Donovan divined this at once.

"He oughtn't to be up here, I know," he began, deprecatingly, "but I can't keep him down, poor fellow! he's always miserable when I'm ill, and the worst of it is he won't obey orders, but thinks it his turn to be master."

"Poor dog!" said Mrs. Tremain, softening towards the offender and venturing to pat him. "He does seem very unhappy about you; it's really wonderful the amount of expression which a dog can put into his face."

"Yes, Waif and I can talk together quite easily; I don't know what I should have done without him, specially when I was laid up; he was often the only nurse I had."

Then a question of Mrs. Tremain's led to an account of his wretched winter, to a discussion of illness in general, to an amusing, though to Mrs. Tremain a somewhat sad description of his various nurses, including poor old Mrs. Doery, both in her character of guardian of the sick and instructor of youth.

"I have not been used to your kind of nursing," he added, after a pause; "you must remember that, and not let me take up your time; I am afraid this dependence will unfit me for the tussle with the world which I must go back to as soon as my ankle is all right."

"You can hardly help being dependent when you can't move," said Mrs. Tremain, smiling.

"No, but it's a training in patience to be helpless and to submit to being muddled, whereas to lie still and be spoilt, humoured, waited on, and amused must surely be demoralising, too pleasant and unusual to fit one for another plunge into the prickles of life."

"Only that life, however hard, can't be all prickles," said Mrs. Tremain. "Don't you think a little spoiling, as you call it, is everyone's due at one time or another? From your own account you have had to 'rough it' a good deal, and this perhaps is your time for trying dependence without all the discomforts you now associate with it. Besides, I daresay you have had your share of waiting on other people, and know that it is the pleasantest work in the world."

Donovan's face changed, and for some minutes he did not speak. Mrs. Tremain saw that her words must have called up some painful remembrance, and Waif too understood perfectly, for he sprang up with his peculiar low whine and began to lick his master's face. What could it be? What painful chord had she unknowingly touched?

A violent start from Donovan caused Waif to jump down from the pillow, and Mrs. Tremain to return from her musing.

"What is it?" she asked.

"I fancied I heard a little child's voice," he said, rather faintly.

"I expect it is Nesta; she is playing in the garden," said Mrs. Tremain.

He did not answer for some minutes, but lay with closed eyes and a strangely rigid face, the only movement being in the hand Waif was licking, which was clenched and unclenched convulsively. At last, shifting his position a little, he looked up again and said, hurriedly,

"Will you let me see her? I am very fond of children."

His voice more than anything told of the severe struggle he had passed through, but, though Mrs. Tremain doubted whether he were fit for it, she did not like to refuse his request. She went to the French window and called the little girl from the lawn.

Four-year-old Nesta came trotting in gleefully, her little rosy face shaded by a white sun hat, her pinafore full of daisies.

"This is your youngest nurse," said Mrs. Tremain, leading her up to the bed.

Nesta looked half timidly at the invalid visitor whom she had heard of; but the moment she caught sight of Waif, all her shyness vanished, and she fairly clapped her hands.

"Oh! mother, mother, what a dear little dog! Is he doin' to stay?"

"Yes, he has come for a long visit," said Mrs. Tremain, lifting her up to the pillow beside Donovan at his special request. Waif allowed himself to be patted and caressed, and played at "trust and paid for" obediently, but he was too low-spirited about his master to show himself off well, and soon crept away from the little girl to the other side of the bed, where he lay with his sad brown eyes fixed on the invalid.

Then Nesta turned her attention to the new visitor, her shyness speedily passing off.

"How drave you look!" she exclaimed, after scrutinizing his face for a minute or two.

Mrs. Tremain and Donovan both laughed, and then the daisies tumbled out of the pinafore, and Nesta, being reminded by the sight of them of daisy-chains which were to have been made, set to work busily, chattering in her quaint unrestrained way meanwhile.

Donovan had won her heart—as he invariably did win the hearts of little children—and the daisy-chain which was to have been for the favourite doll was now destined for him.

"It will look very pretty, you know, on your white night-down," she said, with her irresistible baby laugh.

Presently, with a puzzled face, came one of her abrupt questions.

"What's 'ou name?"

But Donovan did not hear, for he was looking abstractedly at her bright eyes, trying to see in them some likeness to Dot. And they were a little like, for, although grey, they were in a transition state, and there was a peculiar shade of brown in the iris which somehow made them like Dot's clear hazel. Moreover, they had in them the same innocence, and even in a slight degree the same look of heaven-taught love.

She repeated her question imperatively.

"What's 'ou name?"

He came back to the present with an effort, and answered, gravely, but gently,

"You must call me Dono."

Nesta softly repeated the unusual name, lingering over it half doubtfully.

"Don—o, Mr. Dono."

It was the first time he had heard his child-name since little Dot's death. He caught Nesta in his arms and kissed her passionately.

"Oh! oh! oh!" shrieked Nesta, thinking it the beginning of a game. "The drate bear's dot me; he's doin' to eat me."

"Not too noisy, my little girl," said Mrs. Tremain, lifting her away. Then, noticing the deathly paleness of Donovan's face, she hastened to add, "I think Mr. Dono has had enough of you to-day. Mother will take you into the garden."

"Dood-bye, Mr. Dono, dood-bye," said Nesta, as she was carried off; but he did not answer.

Mrs. Tremain was a few minutes out of the room; when she came back she found Waif in great distress, for what had come to his master he did not know. Donovan had buried his face in the pillow, and, almost for the first time in his life, was crying like a child.

Four years ago Mrs. Tremain had had all her sympathy called out for the reserved un-demonstrative stranger whom she had visited in his bereavement; love and tact had given her power then, they gave her power now. She listened as only a mother could have listened to the story of little Dot, gently drawing Donovan on by her perfect sympathy, until there was little that she did not know of those past times. How it all began, how it was possible for her to win him to speak the name that for months had not passed his lips, cannot be written or explained here. But those who have known a real mother will understand at once, and those who deem it impossible must be "Donovans" themselves, to whom sooner or later like sympathy will be given if it is needed.

And yet, in spite of Mrs. Tremain's present feelings, she had at first not been without a certain shrinking from Donovan—from close knowledge of a professed atheist. Away from him this shrinking had increased. It was not until she was brought face to face with his individuality, till he was essentially Donovan to her, not merely a strange visitor, that it was possible for love to take its right place. But her husband's prophecy was true, and before the day was over she had quite taken the invalid guest into her mother's heart, and only loved him better for his poverty of soul and body.

Class judgment, sweeping condemnation, are for the world,—its ways of dealing with its outcasts; and though the ways are neither good for condemners nor condemned, they will probably last through this age. But there are a few people who are bold enough to defy the world's opinion, and to set at naught the world's ways, because they have the way of Christ ever before them, because they love the ignorant and sinning first, and by reason of that love hate only the ignorance and sin that have led them astray.

Even gentle and loving Mrs. Tremain had hitherto gone with the world in thinking of atheists as a class to be shunned and avoided, rather than as so many members of the great human brotherhood who had fallen into a grievous mistake, and to whom all possible justice, and love, and brotherliness must be shown. Mrs. Causton, good as she was, still failed to see the need of this.

"If a man voluntarily cuts himself off from religion, how is it possible to treat him as a brother?" she argued.

Mrs. Tremain, being but newly persuaded herself of the possibility, did not answer, but looked to her husband.

And the doctor answered in his quiet way:

"I never could see the difficulty of that; for

the Fatherhood of God seems to me to answer it all. Universal fatherhood causes universal brotherhood, and the one is as really unalterable as the other. That we do not see it to be so is surely our own fault. As a rule, though, it is only those who believe that God ever ' gives up ' souls, who treat men as outcasts. They are quite logical in doing so. But, once believe that 'lost' means 'not found yet,' that the Good Shepherd seeks the sheep '*until* He finds it,' that the Fatherhood is for ever and ever— and then the fact that your brother is mistaken will only make you love him, and try to show your love to him the more."

Mrs. Causton was silent, for Dr. Tremain had touched on a subject upon which they had long ago agreed to differ. She knew she was one of the "logical" people, and yet, in her heart, she half inclined to the doctor's loving breadth. She also began to revolve in her mind schemes for "converting" the stranger.

Meanwhile, apart from all discussions, and shielded from Mrs. Causton's well-meaning but somewhat mistaken schemes by his continued imprisonment, Donovan spent the most peaceful week of his life. There was something indescribably restful in the atmosphere of Trenant, a refinement about the daily small-talk, an entire absence of that perpetual sitting in judgment on neighbours and acquaintances, which goes far to make the conversation in many families, a peculiar quickness and readiness to perceive humour, and a perfect understanding of that delicious family teazing which is certainly the salt of home life. Though prevented by his invalidism from coming into the very centre of all this, Donovan yet felt much of it in his sick-room. Of Gladys he saw little, but Mrs. Tremain was constantly with him. Jackie and Nesta were always ready to enliven him when he grew dull, and the doctor gave him all his spare time, bringing his microscope, or his fossils for arranging and sorting, or any of his hundred and one naturalist hobbies, and turning the sick-room into something between a museum and an untidy workshop.

Donovan's love deepened day by day, he could have lain in contented silence for hours, just watching the doctor at his work, and though they generally had plenty of animated talk together, it was no necessity to him. The delight of knowing any man whom he could absolutely and unreservedly trust was in itself absorbing, and there was much besides. Mrs.

Tremain, whom he admired and loved scarcely less, and to whom he talked more, influenced him in a way quite as much as her husband. Having once spoken to her of Dot, he now continually returned to the subject, for he felt there was not the danger in thinking of the past that there had once been, and daring to let it all come back to him, he was able to realise that memory is indeed a priceless possession. Then, too, in this week there came to him, almost for the first time, a flickering shadow of doubt in one of his most positive convictions. He had looked on Christianity as a creed which could not be connected with any practical kindliness of life; it had seemed to him merely a sort of *sauve qui peut*. Now at Trenant there was none of the conventional religion to which he was only too well accustomed, but he found himself constantly reminded, in the small concerns of daily life, of that historical Christ for whose character he had conceived the greatest admiration. Little or nothing was *said*, but Donovan felt that he was in a perfectly new atmosphere. Whether these Tremains were living under a delusion, of course he could not say; he did not wish even to think just now.

Strange, dreamy, delicious days! often afterwards in the heat and struggle of life he looked back to them, and always associated with them in his mind were snatches of "In Memoriam," which, in spite of his assurances of an utterly unpoetical temperament, Mrs. Tremain read to him. He had spoken quite truly, there were very few poems which could touch him, but the "living poem" of childhood, and this one great song of immortality, took possession of his very being. The thin green volume was always near his bed—he soon knew most of it by heart.

Meanwhile, Dr. Tremain, seeing that his patient grew stronger in body and evidently happier in mind, began to dread more and more the broaching of that distasteful subject which was constantly in his thoughts. He was of course, however, too wise and too true a friend to put it off long; and at the end of the week, when his patient was well enough to be moved to a sofa and be wheeled into the breakfast-room, he made an opportunity for the private talk which must reveal to Donovan all his step-father's treachery.

The sofa had been placed by the open window, and Donovan was enjoying, as only an invalid can enjoy, the delights of a thorough change; his face was particularly bright and contented when Dr. Tremain came in from his afternoon visits in Porthkerran, with his mind made up to his disagreeable task; it was therefore all the harder to speak, but the doctor knew he had no right to delay any longer, and sitting down near his guest he began with but little preamble.

"Are you up to a business talk this afternoon? If so, I want to speak to you about a matter which has been troubling me very much for the last week—since the night you came, in fact."

"A talk about your business, I suppose," said Donovan, "for I, as I told you, am simply penniless, so my affairs don't admit of much discussion."

"You are mistaken," said the doctor. "You ought not to be penniless, and it is solely with regard to your affairs that I have been so troubled. I should have spoken to you before, but I waited till you were stronger."

Donovan looked perplexed; the doctor continued:

"You told me the other day that your father's will left everything, unconditionally, to your mother, did you not?"

"Certainly, or else I could not be in my present straits."

"And you ought not to be," said the doctor, unable to speak as quietly as he wished. "Donovan, before Colonel Farrant's death he made and I witnessed another will, by which the property was left to you, your mother of course being——"

His sentence was never finished, for Donovan started up, his face white and set, but with a sort of fierce light about it.

"What?" he gasped, "that villain destroyed it, then! Tell me more—quickly—who witnessed it? when was it made?—I recollect nothing. Are you sure—*sure?*"

"That it was legally correct, I am certain," said the doctor; "but do try to quiet yourself or I shall never be able to explain it to you."

"I am quiet," said Donovan, lying back again with a marble face. "Go on, please; only let me hear all—and I'll not interrupt."

"The afternoon your father died," resumed the doctor, "I came, as you know, about three o'clock to visit him. He was very much worried, for Mr. Turner the lawyer, whom he specially wished to see, was away, and he told me that knowing his danger, that he might really die at any minute, he was anxious to make his will at once, so that all might be left straight for you. He explained to me that his former will had been made just after his marriage, and that he thought it wiser to make a fresh one. Of course worry was the very worst thing for him, and, in order that he might be at rest about it, I suggested that he should make his own will temporarily, till a lawyer was at hand, and that seemed to relieve him at once. Do you remember that I came to the head of the stairs and called you?"

"Perfectly," replied Donovan, speaking with difficulty. "You asked for a sheet of writing-paper. I brought it to you."

"Yes, and on that paper, at Colonel Farrant's direction, I wrote words to the effect that he desired to bequeath all his property to you. That an ample allowance—I cannot recall the exact amount—was to be made to Mrs. Farrant, and that Mr. Ellis Farrant was to be the sole executor. I remember he hesitated some time about that, and tried to think of some one else who could also be executor; he said that the second named in his former will had lately died. Thinking it, however, only a temporary thing, he left Mr. Ellis Farrant's name alone."

"The witnesses?" asked Donovan.

"Myself and a servant, Mary Pengelly, who is dead"

"Dead!" he exclaimed, a dark shade passing over his face. "Then it's all up with me; the will can't be proved."

"I half fear not," said the doctor, "though it seems not so impossible as I at first thought. Directly I learnt your name and saw what must have happened I wrote to a solicitor I know in town, and gave him all the circumstances—of course, without names. He allowed that a case might be made for you—such a thing has been done before now. Your recollection of having fetched the sheet of paper might go for something, but the cost of a lawsuit would be enormous, and the result, of course, doubtful. I blame myself very much now for not having taken steps to see that the will was proved. A year or two afterwards, when we were in town, I did half think of it when I happened to pass Somerset House; but some chance meeting prevented me. If I had only had more insight! But I never dreamt of suspecting treachery in Mr. Farrant."

"No, he is too bland, too clever, too consummate a hypocrite!" replied Donovan, bitterly. "No one suspects him. He took the will from you, I suppose, and showed all proper feeling, and none of his blackguardism."

"I gave him the will directly after your father's funeral. He took it quite unconcernedly; I noticed nothing the least remarkable in his manner. If only some one else had been present! If only I'd had the sense to be more cautious!"

"Don't blame yourself," said Donovan, his face softening at once. "That would be just the one thing I couldn't bear. It was no manner of fault of yours; if it had been, it would be easy to put up with—I could endure anything from you. But that traitor, that villain, who all the time is looking as smug and proper as can be, who gives *my* money to charities, who makes merry in *my* house, who goes to church and calls himself a "miserable sinner," and asks for mercy that he may go on comfortably! How can you expect me to think religion anything but a miserable sham, the veriest farce?"

There was a minute's silence when he paused, and, before the doctor had ventured any answer to this very natural outburst, the door opened, and Gladys came in, her hands full of blush-roses and seringa.

"I have brought you some flowers," she said, crossing the room to the sofa. "You must not be cheated of your daily nosegay because you are getting better."

Nothing could have quieted Donovan so effectually as this interruption; he watched in silence while Gladys arranged the flowers. Very pure and fresh and flower-like she looked herself; she fascinated him utterly.

When she left the room again he was the first to speak.

"Forgive me for what I said just now," he began, looking at the doctor with the light of indignation in his eyes softened down to sadness. "I was very wrong to mock at the religion you believe in. This last week you have almost made me think there may, after all, be such a thing as Christianity, I believe for you, at any rate, there is such a thing. But the thought of Ellis Farrant made me mad! You must remember it is only *that* kind of religion I have met with till now—that injustice and loathing and discourtesy are, with scarcely an exception, all that I've received from religious people."

"God forgive them!" exclaimed the doctor. Then, after a pause, "But what I can't understand is the systematic way in which Mr. Farrant must have managed everything. A sudden act of passion I can understand, but deliberately to plan and calculate another's ruin——"

Donovan's face suddenly crimsoned.

"Stop!" he cried "Don't say you can't have pity on such meanness. Remember what I used to be!"

"Your circumstances go far to excuse you," were the words which trembled on the doctor's lips, but he wisely kept them back, and did not break in upon the perfectly natural and right shame by any speech. Instead he just put his strong, firm hand on Donovan's.

After a long silence Donovan looked up once more. He seemed to have mastered the situation now, all indignation and agitation of manner had left him, and Dr. Tremain was struck by the sense and coolness with which he spoke.

"The next thing to be thought of is, what

can we do? A lawsuit seems out of the question, but I don't think that for that reason I need sit still and do nothing to right myself. Shall I send a letter to Ellis Farrant, and just tell him that I have learnt all from you?"

"I think, if you don't object," said the doctor, "it would be much better for me to go to Oakdene Manor and see Mr. Farrant. A letter can be simply ignored, but if I can once see him I shall at least get some definite answer from him. Will you consent to that?"

"It would of course be the best chance for me," said Donovan. "Only I can't endure that you should have the trouble and annoyance."

"You think it is all like a game of 'neighbour, I'm come to torment you,'" replied the doctor, laughing. "You having come to me, and I being on my way to Mr. Ellis Farrant!"

"Well, I've given you nothing but trouble yet," said Donovan. "And this horrid business will hinder you and take you away from home."

"My dear Donovan," said the doctor, still laughing, "you are so exceedingly unlikely ever to be a busybody that I'll venture to give you this maxim, 'Thy business is mine, and mine thine, if there's the ghost of a chance that we can either of us help the other.' Besides, have I not told you that we don't allow units in Cornwall? We're a joint-stock company, and as long as you are here you must put up with all the seeming eccentricities of the 'one and all' system."

The doctor being pretty free that week, it was arranged that he should go to Greyshot the following day, in the hope of getting an interview with Ellis Farrant. As soon as all was settled he left the room to speak to his wife, and to make arrangements for his absence, while Donovan lay in what seemed almost strange calmness.

He had learnt that the Manor was his by right, that there was but a small chance of his getting it; he had also learnt that his step-father's injustice had been far greater than he had hitherto imagined; but then the repentance for his own past was growing more real and strong each day, and his belief in goodness and purity and love was struggling into life—his patience was perhaps, after all, not so strange!

In the midst of this home, with its love, and peace, and breadth of sympathy, his frozen heart was expanding. That very afternoon he had taken the first step towards forgiveness, he had placed himself on a level with his step-father, had not shrunk from admitting that he too had offended in much the same way. And strong in his possession of love—this new strange family love—he waited for what the future should bring, while in the present all went on quietly, the very sounds of life seeming full of peace. The gardener mowing the lawn, the birds singing in the shrubbery, the children laughing at their play, and from the next room Gladys' voice singing as she worked; he did not know her song, but the refrain reached him through the open window.

> "And truth thee shall deliver,
> It is no drede!"

CHAPTER X.

OAKDENE MANOR.

> Oh, righteous doom, that they who make
>   Pleasure their only end,
> Ordering the whole life for its sake,
>   Miss that whereto they tend.
>
> While they who bid stern duty lead,
>   Content to follow, they,
> Of duty only taking heed,
>   Find pleasure by the way.
> ARCHBISHOP TRENCH.

FOR more than a year Ellis Farrant had reigned supreme at Oakdene Manor, but, in spite of every effort to enjoy himself and stifle his conscience, he had been exceedingly miserable. In the winter after Mrs. Doery's return from nursing Donovan, he worked himself up into such a state of nervous terror that, had he possessed a trifle more resolution, he would probably have confessed his crime and sought Donovan out at Monaco. But he was weak, deplorably weak, and so he lived on at the Manor, a misery to himself and to everyone else. He interrogated the housekeeper closely as to his step-son's means of living, asked her endless questions about him, and received somewhat curt answers, for Doery felt bound to take the part of her ne'er-do-weel. Moreover she brought him back all the money which he had given her to use for the invalid, with an assurance that Mr. Donovan would not touch it, had been very angry with her for trying to persuade him to pay the doctor's bill with it, and had said that Mr. Farrant must salve his conscience in some other way.

Poor Ellis! it really had relieved him a little to send those two ten-pound notes to his victim, and to have them thrown back in his face seemed hard; they made him feel uncomfortable for days. At last he put them in the church plate and was at ease again.

But his remorse having only reached the stage of desiring the personal comfort of restitution, it was scarcely wonderful that when a chance of honest confession was given him he rejected it. He cared nothing for Donovan, he only wanted to enjoy the sense of innocence again, to escape from the horrible dread of future punishment which perpetually haunted his poor, selfish soul. Naturally enough remorse on such a basis was like the house built upon the sand, and when, one afternoon in July, a card was brought into the smoking-room bearing the words—" Dr. Tremain, Trenant, Porthkerran," Ellis, half crazy with terror, was driven to take refuge in cunning.

The doctor meanwhile waited in the drawing-room, involuntarily taking stock of this place which by right belonged to his patient, and struggling to keep his indignation within bounds, that he might be cool enough for the coming interview. But he was not at all prepared for the manner of his reception.

The door opened, the master of the house came forward with outstretched hand, an easy-mannered country gentleman, full of genial hospitality; this was the character which Ellis desired to assume, and he acted his part splendidly.

" I think I have had the pleasure of meeting you before, Dr. Tremain," he said, in a hearty voice. " Delighted to see you, sir; I assure you we have none of us forgotten your courtesy at the time of my poor cousin's death. Are you staying in the neighbourhood?"

"I came solely for the purpose of seeing you," said the doctor, gravely. "Mr. Farrant, you seem to have some remembrance of our meeting at Porthkerran, after Colonel Farrant's death. Excuse the seeming impertinence, but have you no remembrance of the Colonel's will which I then placed in your hands?"

There was not a trace, not the smallest sign of guilt in Ellis's face. He raised his eyebrows, and for a moment stared blankly at the doctor.

"My good sir, I am quite ready to excuse all seeming impertinence, but I am utterly at a loss to understand your meaning."

"Your memory must be capricious," said the doctor. "Do you recollect your cousin's funeral?"

"Certainly," replied Ellis, with all due dignity.

"Do you recollect that, after the funeral, we returned to the inn, and that I then gave you a sheet of paper, on which Colonel Farrant had made his will, under circumstances which I described to you?"

A light as of dawning perception began to steal over Ellis's face.

"Ah! now I know to what you refer!" he exclaimed. "Forgive my apparent forgetfulness. I assure you it was not forgetfulness of your services, but merely of the business transaction. Yes, I remember perfectly now. It was a codicil, which, I believe, you yourself witnessed, and in which my cousin left a legacy to a comrade of his out in India."

"Mr. Farrant, seeing that I wrote the will from the Colonel's dictation, you must at once see that it is useless to evade the truth in this way," said Dr. Tremain, controlling his temper with difficulty: "The will directed that this property should be bequeathed to Donovan Farrant, the Colonel's only son; and I am here to-day to demand of you why he is not in possession of it."

"My dear sir, you are labouring under a most extraordinary delusion," said Ellis, with a smile. "You are most entirely mistaken. But, putting that aside, I really may have the right to ask why you intrude into my personal concerns. You are almost a stranger to me, and, though I shall be delighted to show you any hospitality in my power, yet, sir, I think you must allow that to establish an inquisition with regard to my private affairs, is, to say the least of it, unusual. As the proverb has it, you know, 'An Englishman's house is his castle,' and though——"

"If it *were* your house," interrupted the doctor, "I should not have intruded myself upon you, but I come now as the representative of the right owner, who lies ill at my own home."

"Oh! the mystery begins to explain itself then," said Ellis. "I am exceedingly sorry for you, Dr. Tremain, but I see now that you have been imposed upon by that miserable step-son of mine. I suppose Donovan has been fabricating this tale? He is a very clever fellow, and no doubt his story was plausible enough."

"You know perfectly well, Mr. Farrant, that Donovan was utterly ignorant of the true facts of the case, and that it was he who learnt them from me, not I from him. Since, however, you so wilfully refuse to acknowledge what you must be aware I know perfectly well, may I ask you to produce this codicil which you speak of, or to prove to me that this legacy was ever paid."

"It never was paid," said Ellis, coolly. "I was, as you remember, named as sole executor, and of course put myself at once in communication with this Indian friend. I can't even recall the fellow's name now. Perhaps you can, having written the codicil. But, poor man, he died of cholera a week before the Colonel's death.

The codicil was of course worthless then, and was, I believe, destroyed. So you see I cannot offer you more proof. Now, if you will excuse me, where is the proof of *your* assertion? Where is your second witness?"

"The second witness of Colonel Farrant's will—Mary Pengelly—is dead," said the doctor; "otherwise, of course, legal proceedings would have been taken against you."

Ellis, immensely relieved, burst out laughing.

"'Pon my word, Dr. Tremain, this really is a most ridiculous affair. You, with no manner of proof, expect me to believe your assertion, and I am in the unfortunate dilemma of having nothing to convince you of my assertion. We might go on arguing till Doomsday, and be no nearer any agreement."

"Yes, I see perfectly well that discussion is useless," said the doctor, very gravely, "but it was my duty to let you know that your doings were discovered. It is also my duty to tell you that Donovan is utterly destitute, and that if something is not——"

He was interrupted by a fresh voice.

"Who is speaking of Donovan?" exclaimed Adela Farrant, suddenly appearing at the open window. She was in her shady hat and gardening gloves, and in passing along the terrace she had caught the name which during the last year had passed into silence like that of little Dot.

"This gentleman has come to see me on business, Adela; I must beg that you do not interrupt us," said Ellis, half forgetting his *rôle*. But Adela was not to be sent away like a child, and her brother's words only made her the more sure that the strange gentleman had brought news of Donovan.

"How is my cousin Donovan?" she asked, boldly, turning to Dr. Tremain. "I am sure I heard you speaking of him."

"Yes, you are quite right," replied Dr. Tremain, rising from his seat. "I was telling Mr. Farrant that Donovan is now staying with me at Porthkerran, that he is utterly without means of subsistence, and that he has had a hard struggle to live honestly; he would have got on well enough if his health had not given way. I have been urging Mr. Farrant to be just to him; but I fear with little success."

"Wait a minute," said Adela, with her usual prompt decision; "wait just one minute." She hurried across the room to the window, and called, clearly and unhesitatingly, "Nora! Nora!"

"I do wish, Adela, you would be more careful!" exclaimed Ellis. "It will agitate Nora dreadfully to hear about Donovan."

"Let it," said Adela, scornfully. "She ought to be agitated."

"I shall not attempt to resume our discussion," said Dr. Tremain, coldly, when Adela went out on to the terrace to meet Mrs. Farrant. "Only I hope you understand the awful responsibility which you incur."

Ellis would have replied, but at that minute Adela returned with her sister-in-law.

Time had dealt kindly with Mrs. Farrant, she was still pretty, languid, gentle, and ladylike; but there was a shade of sadness in her face now which had never been seen in past days. Considering the unusual circumstances, her manner was marvellously composed, however, as she gave her hand to the doctor.

"Miss Farrant tells me you have news of my son," she said, in her calm voice. "I hope he is well?"

Dr. Tremain was so annoyed at the apparent want of feeling that he answered, almost sharply,

"No, madam, he is anything but well; twice this year he has been at death's door. He came to me a week ago penniless and half starving."

The next minute he almost regretted that he had spoken with such impetuosity, for he saw that after all she had something of a mother's heart hidden away in folds upon folds of self-love. Her eyes dilated.

"No, no!" she cried. "You must be mistaken; it surely can't be my son! Donovan ill—Donovan starving! Oh! Ellis, you must have pity on him—you must help him!"

"My dear Nora, I have offered to help him before now, and he flung the money back in my face," said Ellis.

"You must remember that in the last week his position towards you is changed," said Dr. Tremain. "That you can leave him in his present straits without help I simply will not believe."

Mrs. Farrant began to question the doctor about her son's illness, allowing more and more of her real love to come to the surface, while Adela went over to her brother and began to remonstrate with him.

"Now, Ellis, do this boy justice, and make him a proper yearly allowance," she urged.

"Give him his £300 a year, and perhaps in time I may come to respect you again. You can't say now that you sent him off in a sudden fit of passion, for here is a chance for you to set all right, and, if you don't take it, you'll be the most mean-spirited of mortals."

Ellis smiled a grey smile. How little Adela knew what setting all right would involve! However, he would do something for his stepson, only not too much, for he had a selfish dread lest Donovan might possibly use the money against him, be tempted to go to law about this will, or in some way make life uncomfortable to him. So with pitiable meanness he scoffed at Adela's £300, and wrote instead an agreement by which he bound himself to pay to his step-son £50 half-yearly.

He gave the promise to Dr. Tremain with as condescending a manner as if he had been bestowing a princely favour, all the time knowing perfectly well that the very chair he sat on belonged to Donovan. Dr. Tremain took the paper without a word, and turned to Mrs. Farrant:

"I cannot say that this will convince Donovan that there is such a thing as truth and justice in the world, but it will do him some good to know that he still has your love, Mrs. Farrant.

You will send him some message, I hope."

Her tears were flowing fast, but she made an effort to check them.

"Tell him I know I failed when we were together, that it was my fault; and oh! do be good to him, Dr. Tremain—make him understand that I do love him."

"I think that message will help him on," said the doctor, warmly. "It is very good of you to entrust it to me. For the rest, I can only say that I will treat him like my own son."

With that he rose to go, but he had scarcely left the house when he was called back. Mrs. Farrant hastened towards him.

"One moment, Dr. Tremain—will you take this to Donovan?" She drew a ring from her finger. "Ask him if he still loves me to wear it; tell him how I have longed to hear of him, how thankful I am for your visit to-day."

"And as for me," exclaimed Adela, coming forward and putting her hand in the arm of her sister-in-law. "Please tell Donovan that I, being a free agent, shall write to him now that I know his whereabouts. I don't see why a freak of my brother's should come between us, and I shall expect him to answer me for the sake of old times."

And so ended Dr. Tremain's visit. He left the Manor with mingled feelings; in one way he had received more than he expected, in another less. But the atmosphere of the place was unspeakably wretched, and the doctor was long in losing his keen impression of it. A loveless home, a treacherous, scheming man for the head of the house, his languid wife, his rather flippant sister; among such influences as these Donovan had grown up. And yet in every one there was some good, entirely latent good in Ellis certainly, but in Mrs. Farrant there was a genuine touch of motherliness, in Adela a certain desire for justice and willingness to befriend the ill-used.

There was, too, one influence which Dr. Tremain had forgotten. He had learnt from his wife the story of little Dot; the sight of the church tower in the valley, with its giant yew-tree and clustering gravestones, reminded him that there had been another member of the Manor household—that Donovan had had at least one ray of heaven's own sunlight in his life. He made his way to the little churchyard, and without much difficulty found Dot's grave; but as he looked down at the marble cross, with its inscription of "I am the resurrection and the life," his thoughts were more of the living Donovan than of the little child who "after life's fitful fever" rested well. How that cross and motto must have mocked him in his hopeless grief!—how he must have dashed his heart against words to him so hollow and meaningless! The awful realisation of what his sorrow must have been came to the doctor overpoweringly; for the first time he fully understood the ever-present look of pain in Donovan's eyes; it was there when he spoke of other things, when he was at ease, even when he was laughing—a look of hunger which could never be satisfied. If anything could have deepened the doctor's love for his guest, it would have been the sight of that hopeless grave. He turned away at last, feeling no longer the oppression of his visit to the Manor, for he was communing with that very Resurrection and Life who alone could lighten Donovan's heart.

It was not till the afternoon of the following day that he reached home. The house was quiet and deserted, but in the garden there were sounds of distant voices, following which the doctor was led to the orchard. There all the home party were gathered together, Mrs.

Tremain working, Gladys reading aloud, Donovan lying on his wheeled couch under the shade of an old apple-tree, and in the background the two little ones at play. They looked so comfortable that he was loth to disturb them, but Jackie in climbing one of the trees caught sight of him, and in a minute, with shrieks of delight, had rushed forward announcing his advent.

Donovan's colour rose a little, but he waited patiently till all the greetings were over; then Gladys put down her book, and by a promised game of hide and seek drew the children away, so that her father might be able to talk uninterruptedly.

"I have not fared well," he began, in answer to the mute inquiry on Donovan's face. "But I have at least seen Mr. Farrant, which is something."

Then he described the interview as well as he could, and Donovan listened without the slightest comment until the doctor spoke of Mrs. Farrant.

"You saw her!" he exclaimed. "I am very glad of that. Tell me more. Was she looking well—happy?"

"Scarcely happy; but then she was naturally upset by hearing of your illness, and of the troubles you have been through."

"You must be mistaken. She never really cared for me; she would never show more than a well-bred interest, and that only because she was listening to a stranger."

"I think, Donovan, *you* are very much mistaken," said the doctor, quietly. "The mistake may be very natural, but I am sure that if you had seen your mother you couldn't for one moment have doubted her love. But stay, I have a message for you."

He repeated Mrs. Farrant's words just as they had been spoken to him. Donovan was touched and surprised.

"Did she really say that!" he exclaimed. "Don't think me too unnatural and hardhearted, but I can scarcely believe it. You are sure those were her words?"

"Quite sure," said the doctor, smiling. "And I bring you substantial proof. I had left the house when she called me back, and begged me to take you this ring of hers, and to ask you, if you still loved her, to wear it. The very last thing she said was, 'Tell Donovan how I have longed to hear from him, and how thankful I am for your visit.'"

"Poor mother! she must be very much

changed," said Donovan, taking the ring, and turning it slowly round in his thin fingers. The stone was a white cornelian, and on it was engraved the Farrant motto. It was a ring which he remembered to have seen on his mother's hand since his childhood.

The doctor watched him a little curiously, for there was some hesitation in his manner as he twisted the ring from side to side. At length, however, he put it on very deliberately, then looking at the doctor he said, with a sigh,

"After all, I am half sorry she has done this. I am afraid it is a sign that she is unhappy in the present, that Mr. Farrant is making her miserable, as I always prophesied he would. I would rather have been without her love, and believed her to be happy, as she was at first after her marriage."

"But supposing the old happiness were false, and that through the disappointment she came to realise the truth?" suggested the doctor.

"The truth—at least, if her love to me is true—can't do her much good, can in fact only make her unhappy," said Donovan. "She will never see me, and of what earthly use is love if you can't do something to prove it by service? That is why I half doubted about wearing this ring; I shall never be able to do anything for my mother. I believe I do love her; but love without service is the ghost of love, hardly worthy the name."

"You are right, I think, in all but one thing," said the doctor. "You can prove your love by this: you *wish* to help your mother, but circumstances prevent you. Supposing that she were left alone in the world; you would be the first to go to her."

"Yes," said Donovan, with emphasis.

"And, besides," continued the doctor, "I don't agree that she does nothing for you. Does she not make the world a better place to you? Is it not something that you can say to yourself, 'I am not cheated of this goodly birthright—I have a mother after all.' Is it not a great thing to know there is some one thinking of you, loving you—perhaps praying for you?"

"I can't do that for her," he replied, in a low voice.

"No, not yet," said the doctor, quietly; and then there was a long silence.

At last Donovan spoke.

"You said that Mr. Farrant promised to make me some sort of allowance. I suppose I'm not bound to accept it?"

"No, but I advise you to do so," said the doctor, unable to help smiling at the very evident look of distaste which his words called up. "You see, to begin with £100 a year is better than nothing—that's the common-sense view; and, from a higher point, I don't think it will do you any harm to endure the discipline of those half-yearly cheques."

Donovan laughed outright.

"I think I see myself writing the receipts every six months in the style of a Greyshot tradesman. 'D. F. with best thanks, and soliciting Mr. Farrant's esteemed patronage for the future.'"

The doctor was not a little relieved to hear such a hearty laugh, he laughed himself, but waited for Donovan to go on with the discussion. With amusement still flickering about his face he continued,

"Still the great question is unsolved, what else am I to do besides eating these half-yearly slices of humble pie?"

"What have you a taste for?" asked Dr. Tremain.

"For nothing in the world except doctoring," said Donovan, with decision. "It has always seemed to me the only sensible and thoroughly satisfactory profession. I suppose it's no good thinking of it though. The training is very long, isn't it?"

"Four years," said Dr. Tremain. "The longest of any of the professions. But if you've a real inclination for it, you should certainly follow your bent. In many ways I think you are well fitted for it."

"Do you really?" exclaimed Donovan. "I was afraid Nature had fitted me for nothing but the work of a mathematician, and I should be afraid to try that now."

"Why?" asked the doctor, surprised at such an admission.

"Because I know I'm as hard as nails already, and don't want to get more so."

"Proverbially, you know, the medical course hardens men, for a time at least, but every rule has its exceptions, and I half fancy you would make an exception to this."

"How about the entrance fees at the hospital?"

"One hundred pounds, but you can pay by instalments. There are many other expenses, though, and you must live meanwhile. I don't quite see how you can do it. However, we will manage it somehow between us. A real inclination such as this ought not to be neglected."

"You have given me enough discipline, though, already," said Donovan. "I can't become utterly dependent. Don't think me ungrateful, but unless I can scrape through on my hundred pounds a year I won't go up. But it must be possible—I'll do it somehow. I suppose there are scholarships, too, at most of the hospitals?"

Upon this ensued a long discussion as to the respective merits of St. Bartholomew's and St. Thomas's, and that evening it was arranged that Donovan should become a student at the latter hospital. His thoughts were successfully drawn from Ellis Farrant and the Oakdene property, by the prospect of going up in two months' time for his preliminary.

CHAPTER XI.

THE IDEAL WOMAN.

> But am I not the nobler through thy love?
> O three times less unworthy! likewise thou
> Art more thro' Love, and greater than thy years.
> The sun will run his orbit, and the moon
> Her circle. Wait, and Love himself will bring
> The drooping flower of knowledge changed to fruit
> Of wisdom. Wait: my faith is large in Time,
> And that which shapes it to some perfect end."
> TENNYSON.

"YOU look very hot and very much bored. Don't you think those great books are too dull for a summer morning?" exclaimed Gladys, coming into the breakfast-room, where Donovan was working, one sunny day in August.

The table was dragged up to his couch, and, to all appearance, he was very busy with his examination work.

"It is not the *big* books that bore me," he said in reply.

"But something has certainly happened to you since breakfast time," said Gladys, laughing. "Can Aunt Margaret have been here?"

There was such *naïveté* in her tone that Donovan could not help laughing.

"Yes," he replied, "Mrs. Causton has been here for the last hour. She is very—kind-hearted."

Gladys smiled.

"Yes, very, but she rubs people the wrong way. Papa says it is because she thinks there is only one way. As if, you know, we were all made alike!"

"I told you it wasn't the big books that bored me," said Donovan. "What do you think of this?" He handed her a little brown volume, and turning to the title-page Gladys read—"An Inquiry into the Nature, Symptoms, and Effects of Religious Declension, with the Means of Recovery."

The colour rose in her cheeks.

"Oh! I am so sorry!" she exclaimed. "I hope—I hope you haven't minded it very much?"

"I've no business to mind it, for she was very kind; but there are some subjects which I had rather have touched reverently. Do you think that kind of spiritual hay-making does much good? that raking up of feelings, that tossing of texts? It's the first time I've come across it."

"Except when you met us in the train that day and auntie gave you the tracts."

Donovan laughed a little at the remembrance.

"Do you know though meeting you that day made me feel very much ashamed of myself; I never can think of those tracts without laughing. The first of mine was 'Are you a drunkard?' and the second 'Are you a swearer?' We had a parrot at our rooms, a capital talker, but like almost all parrots, it did swear most dreadfully; some one fastened these tracts to its cage, and taught it to ask the questions—a very wicked thing, wasn't it? but irresistibly comic."

"Poor Aunt Margaret! what would she say!" exclaimed Gladys.

"It is not tracts that are wanted," continued Donovan; "beautiful lives are the best arguments, the only ones which will ever influence me."

"Lives like your little sister's," said Gladys, gently.

"Yes," he replied; then, after a pause, "Not

that her life was what some people would have approved; she never thought much of what is called the soul, she was a little Undine till she was nearly thirteen."

"Was she thirteen when she died? I had fancied her younger somehow."

"So she was really in mind and ways," he said, quietly. "She was a thorough child; your little Nesta reminds me of her, though I don't suppose you would see any likeness."

He took the little miniature out and placed it in her hands. Gladys looked at it in silence; it was a most beautiful child's face, with delicate features, clear, pale complexion, arched and pencilled eyebrows, and glorious hazel eyes— eyes which she thought very much like Donovan's, only they were entirely without the sadness which lurked in his.

"Thank you so much for letting me see it," she said, giving it back to him. "She must have been far lovelier than little Nesta; but I think I do see the likeness you mean. Was this taken long before she died?"

"No, only a few months before," replied Donovan. "It was taken when we were staying at Codrington, and she was just beginning to puzzle herself over all the unanswerable questions; we talked one day about death, and of course I had no comforting things to tell her about it, I couldn't tell her what I believed to be untrue. Then for a time the thought of it haunted us both; there was an artist staying in the hotel, and I got him to do this miniature for me, knowing that the separation must come some day, but not dreaming that it would be so soon."

"And did she ever learn that death is not an endless separation?" asked Gladys, the tears welling up into her eyes.

"Yes," he answered, quietly; "she learnt all that could make her happy, how I don't know. Isn't it strange how easily belief comes to some? I would give worlds to be able now to believe what you believe, to feel certain that I'd got hold of the real truth, but I cannot, it's an impossibility."

"Oh! don't say that," said Gladys, quickly, "leave yourself at least a hope, or how will you ever have the heart to go on searching for the truth? It may not always seem impossible to you."

Her sweet, eager face, with its entire absence of self-consciousness, took Donovan's heart by storm; hitherto she had influenced him, fascinated him, but now for the first time he knew that he loved her.

"Life is full of strange surprises," he answered; "you may be right, I'll unsay that 'impossible.'"

Then with the strange new sense of love in his heart, and the craving for her sympathy, he told her all about Dot's death, and Gladys' tears fell fast as she heard the details of that last night, and realised how terribly Donovan must have suffered.

From that time there was a great difference in their intercourse; they talked much more freely, gliding into a sort of brotherly and sisterly intimacy; at least, so it seemed. Donovan, though conscious of his love, was not in the frame of mind to think of the future, it was quite enough for him to live in the present, knowing and loving Gladys; and she, beginning with the wish to give him a little of the sister's love which he missed so much, drifted imperceptibly, unconsciously into a love altogether different.

Very happy to both of them were those summer weeks; in the long mornings Donovan worked hard for his examinations, in the afternoon there were merry gatherings in the shady old orchard, games with the children, reading aloud, or attempts at sketching.

One afternoon, when they were all sitting in the shade of the great mulberry-tree, engrossed in their own various books, Gladys looked up laughing.

"Just listen to this. How would you have liked it? 'He was constantly annoyed by being asked to write his likes and dislikes in ladies' albums.'"

"I know the horrid inventions," said Donovan. "A cousin of mine used to be always boring people to write in hers—their ideas of pleasure, pain, beauty, and so on."

"Rather fun too, I think," said Gladys. "Only that one's ideas would be always changing."

"I should have no difficulty in writing some of my ideas now," said Donovan. "The idea of happiness would certainly be 'a sprained ankle at Trenant,' and the idea of beauty, 'the long grass and daisies in this orchard with the sunshine on them.'" He added, in his thoughts, "And Gladys sitting with her book among the daisies."

Sometimes, in the cool of the evening, they used to drive out in the pony-chaise, along by the sea, or through the narrow lanes with their high, mossy banks, pausing now and then at some cottage to leave a message, or to visit some of Mrs. Tremain's innumerable friends among the poor. There was very little society round Porthkerran. In the winter Gladys sometimes went to one or two dances at some distant country house. In the summer there was an occasional picnic or garden-party, but the neighbourhood was thinly populated, and the distances were too great for very much visiting. So Porthkerran formed a little clan of its own; and as by good chance the squire and the rector were both fond of natural history, Dr. Tremain was able to gather round him a small scientific society; this, with the exception of the constant visits of Mrs. Causton, and of their nearest neighbour, a jocose old man, Admiral Smith, constituted the clan proper. But the Tremains knew almost everyone in the little fishing-town, and though Gladys never undertook formal district-visiting, she was welcomed in any house, and there was scarcely a child in the place whom she did not know at least by name.

She was therefore never idle and never dull. There were always plenty of tragedies and comedies going on among her large circle of friends, in both of which she was interested.

Or there were orphans to be sent to school, or blind people to be read to, or twin babies who must be worked for, or sick children to be amused. Donovan liked to watch her busy life; she evidently enjoyed it so thoroughly.

There was one event, too, which was constantly being talked of, namely, Dick's return from sea. He was expected in September, and Donovan used to listen half sadly to the daily hopes and wonders as to his progress. When the papers came, there was always a rush to find the latest "Shipping Intelligence," and delighted exclamations when H.M.S. *Cerberus* was mentioned as having left some port on her homeward journey. How strange it must be to be loved, and watched, and waited for so eagerly!

By this time the first cheque from Ellis had been received and acknowledged, and immediately Donovan made use of the money to recover Dot's clock from the Liverpool pawnbroker's. He also sent a ten-pound note to the hospitable Devonshire man who had helped him out of the Foxtor mire. This last piece of gratitude was perhaps slightly rash, considering his very narrow means, but he could not rest till he had sent it.

His ankle was now quite recovered, and in

September he was able to go up for his examination, but not before he had promised to spend his last few days at Porthkerran. The doctor had proposed that he should share Stephen Causton's rooms in town. Stephen was still at St. Thomas's, and as his mother made no objection, and Donovan liked the thought of being with any connection of the Tremains, the arrangement was made; but unfortunately Stephen, who had been spending the vacation abroad, returned with his eyes in a very delicate state, and a bad attack of ophthalmia ensuing, obliged him to give up all thoughts of work for many months.

After his long stay at Trenant, Donovan felt rather at sea when he went up to town to begin his solitary life again. However, he had no time to be dull, for he was very anxious about his examination. Besides, before many days he hoped to be with the Tremains again. He passed his preliminary successfully. The scholarship examination was not till after the beginning of term, so there was nothing to detain him longer, and another week at Gladys' home was not to be missed on any consideration. He went back to Porthkerran in excellent spirits. It was about half-past five on a bright September afternoon when he reached St. Kerrans, the nearest station. He had only just set out for the five-mile walk along the dusty road, when he was overtaken by a fellow pedestrian, who, on seeing the direction he took, hurried after him.

"Are you going beyond Porthkerran?" he inquired.

"No, to Porthkerran itself," replied Donovan, looking at the speaker with some curiosity. He was apparently about his own age, a lithe, active-looking fellow, with a very sunburnt but good-looking face, and merry, blue-grey eyes.

"Let me send your bag with my traps, then; the carrier leaves in an hour's time."

There was a very evident "Who are you?" in Donovan's eyes; but the stranger, nothing daunted, took the bag from him and ran back to the little inn; then, returning in a moment, he said, apologetically,

"You must excuse this 'hail fellow well met' business, but I am Dick Tremain, and, if I am not very much mistaken, you are Mr. Farrant."

They shook hands.

"You are a very clever guesser," said Donovan. "I ought to have known you; but I had no idea you were expected to-day."

"I'm not, that's just the fun of it," returned Dick, accommodating his seaman's gait to Donovan's long strides. "They don't the least expect me; we got into Plymouth Sound this morning, and I made up my mind to come straight on and surprise them. They're all right at home, I suppose?"

"Yes, when I left they were all very well."

"And your ankle is mended again, to judge by the pace you're going at. I heard all about that cliff adventure."

"It brought me the pleasantest two months of my life," said Donovan. "I'm coming down now to say good-bye before starting at St. Thomas's, in October. I'm sorry, though, that I just chanced to come back on the same day you did."

Dick laughed.

"I might take that as a bad compliment, and you know we have still four miles to walk. But in all seriousness you really must take back your words, for I have been particularly hoping to see you, and at Trenant it is always 'the more the merrier.' So you are going to St. Thomas's? Is Stephen Causton still there?"

"Yes; we were to have shared rooms, but

his eyes have given out, so he won't go up this term."

"Better luck for you, I should say. Perhaps you've seen him, though?"

"No, he's only just home. What sort of a fellow is he?"

"A regular sawney—good-humoured enough, but weak as water. He's never been allowed to shift for himself; he's a regular mother's son."

This was a genus utterly unknown to Donovan; he asked several questions about the Caustons, and, as Dick possessed the genial manner and the ready speech of his family, the five mile walk was quite sufficient to make the two pretty well acquainted. At last they reached the turn in the road which brought them into sight of the little fishing-town.

Porthkerran was a very picturesque place; it stood at the head of a tidal inlet, which in olden times had been one of the most frequented harbours of the west. The building of the breakwater had, however, caused it to be superseded by Plymouth Sound, and Porthkerran was now obliged to content itself with seeing from afar the passing ships. It had been a noted resort of smugglers, and the irregularly-built streets, with their narrow twistings and windings, the innumerable passages and mysterious flights of steps, the houses with their second doors and secure hiding-places, all bore witness to the bygone times when the one interest, excitement, and object in life of the inhabitants had been to smuggle, and to escape from the coastguardsmen. Many curious stories were still handed down in the village of great-grandmothers who had concealed fabulous numbers of silk dresses under their own ample skirts; of perilous escapes down dark alleys; of kegs of brandy which some daring sexton had once concealed for several days in the church itself. The rising generation listened with interest to these tales of the evil deeds of their forefathers; sometimes they even went so far as to wish that their own lot had been cast in those more exciting days, and were so depraved as not to

"Thank the goodness and the grace
Which on their birth had smiled."

But to wish that they had not been taught so very often in Sunday-school that the boys who stole apples invariably came to a bad end, or that living in those benighted days they might have enjoyed in peace a little of the excitement of smuggling.

But Porthkerran was now an eminently respectable fishing village, and if it did break the Ten Commandments, broke them in a less flagrant and open manner than in former times. Adulteration of food and false weights were certainly not quite unknown in the place, but on the whole Porthkerran had decidedly improved, and the inhabitants were, as a rule, hospitable, kindly, and staunch.

The little place looked especially pretty in the sunset glow of the September evening; the quaint, compact little town, with its curling columns of blue smoke, telling of the supper in preparation for the fishermen, the narrow strip of beach, dotted here and there with brown nets spread out to dry, the calm bay, with its orange-sailed boats, and aslant from the west a broad pathway of tawny gold, ever, as the sun sank lower, deepening to crimson.

And this was Gladys' home! Donovan's heart gave a great bound when he realised how near he was to her. It was a beautiful little place certainly, but he would have thought the Black Country beautiful if Gladys had lived there. How he had pictured it all to himself up in those dull London lodgings!—how he had paced in imagination that very road, had reached that ivy-covered house! Well, here he was in sober reality, and even as they drew near the door was thrown open, and Gladys' own fresh voice was ringing in his ears.

"Dick—oh! Dick, you dear, delightful boy to come so unexpectedly! How exactly like you to walk in so quietly! And Donovan, too! How clever of you to find each other out!"

Donovan felt the real welcome of her voice and hand; it was, moreover, the first time she had directly spoken to him by his Christian name, for, though he had long ceased to be "Mr. Farrant" to any of them, these two had as yet kept instinctively to that most indefinite of all personal pronouns, "you."

In a minute all the household came flocking out into the hall to welcome the sailor after his long absence. Donovan watched the greetings with a strange mixture of pain and pleasure, his new nature sharing in the general happiness, his old nature viewing all with silent, deep-seated envy. His usual helper, however, came to his aid; a delighted cry of "Dono! Dono!" made him look up, and there, slowly coming down the broad oak staircase, her right foot solemnly stumping in front, her left foot following with less dignity in its wake, was little Nesta.

"Dear Dono to tum back!" she cried, gleefully. "Lift me over the ban'sters, Mr. Dono, up on to you shoulder."

He lifted her across, received a half-strangling hug, and was not a little flattered that only from her perch on his shoulder would she be induced to kiss the strange brother.

After the seven o'clock dinner was over, Donovan made his escape from the rest of the family, strolled down the garden, and gave himself up to a rather sombre reverie. The last words he had heard spoken by Dick to Gladys rang rather painfully in his ears—"Oh, and don't you remember——" There was no one in all the world to whom *he* could now say, "Don't you remember." He had to an almost morbid extent, too, the dread of intruding himself where he was not wanted, and this evening he argued to himself logically enough that it was impossible they should not prefer his absence. And it certainly was true that for a time no one missed him, that the father and mother were entirely engrossed in their boy, that even Gladys did not at first understand his non-appearance. But, delighted as she was at Dick's return, and interested as she was in his stories, she was nevertheless conscious of an undefined sense of trouble, which grew and grew, until at length it flashed upon her suddenly that Donovan must be purposely keeping aloof, afraid of spoiling the freedom of the family talk. She remembered now that she had been talking to Dick as they left the dining-room; how inconsiderate she had been! how absorbed in her own happiness! It was just like Donovan to take himself off alone. He must be found and taken to task. She would not disturb her father or mother, but putting down her work, she slipped quietly out of the room, looked into the study, but he was not there, into the dining-room, but it was empty and deserted, finally snatching up an old wide-awake of her father's as protection from the dew, she instituted a search in the garden.

At last in the twilight she caught sight of a dark figure pacing to and fro by the strawberry beds. He did not notice her till she was almost close to him, then suddenly turning round he found himself face to face with a white-robed apparition, and started a little.

"I'm not a ghost, though I have a white

frock," she exclaimed; "and I'm not papa, though I have his hat. Why are you wandering up and down the very froggiest and toadiest path in the garden?"

"Birds of a feather flock together," he said, lightly. "I've a good deal in common with the frogs, a love of croaking and a coldness of heart—or absence of heart altogether, is it?"

"I came to scold you," said Gladys, "not to laugh. Why have you not been listening to Dick? You've no idea what adventures he has had this voyage."

"Why are *you* not with him?" returned Donovan. "I hoped—I thought you would all forget that I was here, and enjoy him to yourselves."

"Why to *ourselves*?"

"Is not that the only way really to enjoy him?"

"Not when you won't be one of the selves. I thought you did really take this as a home."

"So I do. Never doubt that, in whatever way I act."

"Then why not act as a part of the home; taking it for granted that we like you to be interested in all our interests. Can't you understand that of course we do?"

He did not answer for a moment, but even in the dim, shady garden-walk Gladys could see how his face lighted up—what a strange new look of rest dawned in his eyes!

"I have believed in neither God nor man," he said at last, "but you have forced me to believe in the latter. Ever since I came here you have been teaching me. If ever I doubt human goodness again, I shall only have to remember that there is such a place as Trenant in the world."

"Then if that is so," said Gladys, smiling, "I shall thank my hat for blowing over the cliffs that day, even though it did give you so much trouble and pain. However, we've wandered from the point. You will come in, won't you? It was so stupid of me not to remember sooner that you would be sure to take yourself off."

He laughed a little.

"You own, then, that it was natural?"

"Not at all; most people would never have dreamt of doing such a thing."

"But you knew that I should," said Donovan, triumphantly gaining the assurance that she understood his character.

"Well, yes," she owned, "I thought it would

be very like you to feel in the way and not wanted."

"Don't be too hard on me for that; you've no idea how I've been shut out of things all my life. No one has ever loved me but a few children and a dog or two."

"Oh, you must not say that!" she exclaimed, in a voice so pained, so unlike itself that it even startled her. "You know—you know that is not true!"

As the words passed her lips, she knew for the first time that her own love for Donovan was no sisterly love, no friendly liking; that brief sentence of his and her own impulsive reply revealed to her the wholly unsuspected depth of her feelings. Had she been aware of this sooner, it would have been utterly impossible for her to run out into the garden to find him, as she had done only a few minutes before in perfect simplicity. It was twilight, that was one comfort; he could not see that her cheeks were glowing with maidenly shame, that she was trembling in every limb. Strange as it may seem, though he loved her, he did not notice her sudden change—that is, it did not at all convey to him the faintest idea that her own love caused that pained tone in her voice. They walked on for a minute or two in silence.

Donovan was the first to speak; she knew by his manner that she had not betrayed herself.

"I was wrong to speak bitterly; this evening's welcome to Porthkerran ought to have reminded me of the love I have found here. One of your father's hand-shakes is worth travelling three hundred miles for."

Gladys turned in the direction of the house.

"And Nesta was so delighted to have you back again. You can't think how fond she is of you; we used to hear her telling Waif long stories about you while you were in London. Nesta's stories are such fun. I think she has a good deal of imagination."

They reached the house as she finished speaking, and finding the drawing-room window open, she went in that way and soon had the satisfaction of seeing Donovan really join the family group.

The mantle of his taciturnity seemed to have fallen instead upon her; before long she slipped out of the room and slowly and dreamily wandered away, she hardly knew whither. This strange new conviction, this consciousness of love, seemed to have transported her into a new world. Presently, finding herself by the night nursery door, she stole softly in, and sat down by Nesta's little bed. The curly brown head nestled down on the pillow, the rosy face half hidden seemed the very picture of peace. And Gladys too, though her face glowed and her eyes shone with the love which had just dawned in her heart, was not otherwise than peaceful; there was a great deal of the child about her still, not a thought of the future had crossed her mind.

"You love him too, little Nesta," she whispered, bending over the sleeping child, "but not as I do. Oh! Nesta darling, can you ever be so happy as I am to-night! Can there possibly be such another for you to love!"

END OF THE SECOND VOLUME.

LONDON: PRINTED BY DUNCAN MACDONALD, BLENHEIM HOUSE.

www.ingramcontent.com/pod-product-compliance
Lightning Source LLC
Chambersburg PA
CBHW030731230426
43667CB00007B/676